D1257598

THE
ECOLOGY
OF WAR

THE
ECOLOGY
OF WAR

ENVIRONMENTAL IMPACTS
OF
WEAPONRY AND WARFARE

SUSAN D. LANIER-GRAHAM

WALKER AND COMPANY
NEW YORK

First published in the United States of America in 1993
by Walker Publishing Company, Inc.

Published simultaneously in Canada by Thomas Allen & Son
Canada, Limited, Markham, Ontario

Library of Congress Cataloging-in-Publication Data
Lanier-Graham, Susan D.
The ecology of war : environmental impacts of
weaponry and warfare / Susan D. Lanier-Graham.
p.   cm.
Includes bibliographical references and index.
ISBN 0-8027-1262-2
1. United States—Armed Forces—Environmental aspects.
2. Military policy—United States. 3. Armed Forces—Environmental
aspects. I. Title.
TD195.A75L36   1993
363.73'1—dc20   92-43568
CIP

Printed in the United States of America

2   4   6   8   10   9   7   5   3   1

Book design by Claire Vaccaro

FOR THE CHILDREN of today, who will become the leaders of tomorrow. May you take the lessons of the past and make them the guidelines for the future. I wish for you the vision to guide us to survival.

CONTENTS

CONTENTS

CONTENTS

ACKNOWLEDGMENTS

The Ecology of War has been possible only through the guidance and assistance of more people than I could ever thank here. Countless people have provided information or pointed me in directions I would not have taken alone.

In particular, I would like to thank Paula Ussery, curator of collections at the Admiral Nimitz Museum, Fredericksburg, Texas, and Charles Franson, a devoted volunteer for the archives at the Nimitz Museum. Although I never met Mr. Franson, he did hours of research for me, for which I am most grateful. Also, thanks to John J. Slonaker, chief of the historical reference branch at the U.S. Army Military History Institute, Carlisle Barracks, Pennsylvania. Mr. Slonaker provided a wealth of information and an excellent facility in which to conduct research. Edward J. Boone, Jr., archivist at the Douglas MacArthur Memorial and Archives in Norfolk, Virginia, provided more materials about the South Pacific than I ever knew existed. In addition, the excellent staff members at MacArthur offered numerous research suggestions and alternatives. The office of Thomas Baca, deputy assistant secretary of defense for environment, was most helpful. In particular, Lieutenant Colonel Gary Thomas and Colonel Ken Cornelius took the time to speak with me at great length and to provide me with in-depth information about the military's past and its changing role in today's world. The people at Aberdeen Proving Ground in Maryland have been most helpful. I have spoken to many people there, and they have always been willing to help or to find someone else who could. The history and public affairs offices at the Air Force Academy have been most helpful and willing to offer technical support. Barbara Butler, coordinator of the Biodiversity Resource Center at the California Academy of Sciences in San Francisco provided me with pages of references and further resources when my research was in the early stages. She provided much of the framework for this project. Another wonderful source of references was the Naval War College in Newport, Rhode Island. Ms. Christine Danieli, reference librarian, sent me several bibliographies that proved invaluable in my research. Burr Heneman of the International Council on Bird Preservation and Brent Blackwelder of Friends of the Earth both provided insights into the Persian Gulf War and helpful suggestions.

The work of Dr. Arthur Westing has been a tremendous resource in preparing this book. Dr. Westing's research has helped lay the foundation for so many other works. His dedication to an often depressing and seemingly hopeless topic has been an inspiration to my work, and he has graciously contributed a foreword to this book.

The staff at Craig-Moffat County Public Library in my hometown of Craig, Colorado, was exceptional. Much of my research was a challenge for them and their ancient computer, but they came through for me.

I need to thank my family for being there to support this overwhelming project. Pat and Joe Graham spent an intensive four weeks with me while I conducted research all over the country. Their help and support was wonderful! They and Ralph and Shirley Lanier have been my moral support and my best cheerleaders. When I was sure it couldn't be done, they told me to keep trying.

A special thanks goes to my editor, Mary Kennan Herbert, and the staff and readers at Walker. Mary's confidence in me and in *The Ecology of War* has been important, and the time devoted to helping make this a worthy project has been remarkable.

Most of all, I need to thank my son, Patrick, and my husband, Bill. Patrick put up with a lot the past couple of years, and he even endured lengthy dinner table conversations about World War II, Agent Orange, and the Persian Gulf. Bill, most of all, made this book possible. Without him, it would never have come together. He has been my main researcher, made hundreds of phone calls, read thousands of pages of manuscripts, government documents, letters, and technical manuals for me, and he has been my support through it all—often even at the expense of his own work. I will forever hear that scratch of his red pen on the paper as he made many suggestions!

This book belongs to so many people who have made it possible. Thanks to you all; I hope it is a message that will reach out to the world.

FOREWORD

A government maintains its armed forces at enormous cost, doing so most commonly for the purpose of protecting itself from enemies, both domestic and foreign, and for otherwise reinforcing its domestic and foreign status and policies. Most of the many national governments in the world maintain substantial armed forces that function through the threat of deadly and destructive violence or—should such threat fail to achieve its purpose—by the actual use of deadly and destructive violence.

Armed forces have been embroiled in combat, both within their own borders and across them, many hundreds of times in the years since World War II. Indeed, dozens of hostile military actions are currently in progress in one place or another, as is always the case. In the vivid words of Arthur Koestler, "The most persistent sound which reverberates through man's history is the beating of war drums. Tribal wars, religious wars, civil wars, dynastic wars, national wars, revolutionary wars, colonial wars, wars of conquest and of liberation, wars to prevent and end all wars, follow each other in a chain of compulsive repetitiveness as far as [we] can remember [our] past, and there is every reason to believe that the chain will extend into the future."

Wars are by their very nature costly in human terms. Combatants and noncombatants alike are killed and maimed in a theater of action or have their lives disrupted by war in numerous other ways. Armed forces are costly not only in times of war but also in times of peace. They are continuously costly in material terms, in financial terms, and in intellectual terms. And as Susan Lanier-Graham's book demonstrates so well, they are especially costly in environmental terms.

Disruption of the environment by any means is becoming an ever more serious issue as human numbers and human aspirations continue to soar into a biosphere of finite size. The betterment of the human condition, and our very survival as a civilized people, depend upon an ability to live in long-term harmony with nature. To that end we must learn to develop sustainably, for the benefit of present and future generations. That is to say, we must be able to harvest the natural resources upon which we depend in a sustainable fashion, and we must be able to discard our multifarious wastes—solid, liquid, and gaseous—in an equally sustainable fashion.

Our inescapable goal of balancing human needs with environmental availabilities is becoming increasingly elusive. Thus, one major component of our strategy to achieve such sustainability must be the elimination of any unnecessary disruptions of the human environment. As *The Ecology of War* illustrates graphically, one way available to us to spare the environment is to reduce, if not prevent, the environmental inroads of the military sector of society. The environmental damage that can be avoided by a shrinkage of the military sector of society refers not only to damage in times of war but also to the interwar periods: to the environmental costs of preparing for each war, of reconstructing after each war; and, more generally, of the continuing costs of maintaining a military infrastructure.

Comprehensive human security has two basic components: social security (with its political, economic, and personal elements) on the one hand and environmental security (with its protection, rational utilization, and sustainable-discard elements) on the other. The two components of comprehensive human security—the social and the environmental—are inextricably intertwined: neither is achievable without the other. One of the real strengths of *The Ecology of War* is that this interconnectedness comes through so clearly. Indeed, I was gratified to see that so much of my work in analyzing the impact of military activities has here been made accessible to the general reader, while at the same time having the book make clear its relevance to society today.

In presenting the environmental damage caused by war as well as by its antecedents and sequelae, *The Ecology of War* provides us with the knowledge necessary at least to reduce this source of environmental insecurity, and thus also of overall human insecurity. The attainment of comprehensive human security for its citizenry is a solemn obligation of any government; and a prerequisite for this is an informed citizenry, made possible by the splendid exposé of the author.

The reader of this book will be drawn to the conclusion that we must finally reject warfare as an acceptable human activity. Such rejection must derive not only from the traditional grounds of morality or ethics but now also because it is one of the few environmentally disruptive activities that can be avoided without compromising some other element of comprehensive human security, such as health or education.

—Dr. Arthur Westing

PREFACE

The Ecology of War has been a challenge for me. It began as a need to know, to synthesize history to make sense of what was going on in the world, specifically in the Persian Gulf, at the time. It has become an obsession. The need to understand this thing called war has become a major force in my life.

I chose to examine American warfare throughout history and the impacts of warfare on the natural environment. It is difficult at times to make clear distinctions between the natural environment and the human environment. What makes up the natural environment is, at times, arbitrary for the nonscientist. There are times in the book when I had to make such choices. If something is not included that you, the reader, believe should have been, it probably was not out of disregard for certain conditions. Any omissions that I made were usually in an attempt to keep the book focused on the natural environment.

I also did not directly address the moral and social questions of warfare and the military. There are few subjects in the world today that can elicit such strong responses and arouse so many emotions so quickly as warfare. Those underlying moral and social dilemmas are, therefore, inherently a part of any book about warfare. However, I did not specifically address these concerns.

Perhaps the issue that was the hardest for me to decide on and to follow through on was determining how to handle the human costs of warfare. I chose to focus solely on the environment and the ecological costs of warfare. This is in no way meant to lessen the impact on human life. The cost of war is incalculable to anyone who has ever lost a loved one to war itself or its aftereffects. Just as the environment has suffered dramatically from such programs as the chemical/biological weapons program or the nuclear weapons program in the United States, so too have there been human costs, civilian as well as military. The fact that the book does not address those human costs in no way minimizes the human suffering caused by such programs.

I believe it is important today, as we approach the twenty-first century, to take a serious look at the military legacy in the United States. Today's technology makes environmental damage much more likely than in the past, and the impacts will probably be far greater and of longer duration than ever before. These facts make it necessary to stop and examine the consequences of military actions before the onset of war. In the end, environmental concerns are human concerns as well. If the natural environment around us cannot survive, we will not survive.

I made simplicity one of the major aims of *The Ecology of War*. I do not want readers young or old to struggle through the book. I want it to be a useful overview of the history, a guide through the problems and some of the solutions.

To make the book easier to follow and easy to refer back to, I divided it into three sections. Part I, Early History of Warfare, provides a brief look into early history. Although the United States has always been a sort of maverick in world affairs, the country's leaders have still drawn from experiences of centuries past that are eerily contemporary. However, since *The Ecology of War* is designed as an overview of American warfare, not the entire world, Part I is brief.

Part II, Modern Warfare, the major portion of the book, is divided into three sections. Chapter 1 covers environmental damage during warfare and follows American warfare chronologically from the American Revolution to the Persian Gulf War. Chapter 2 explores environmental impacts following warfare and focuses on several major categories of environmental impacts. Chapter 3 looks at environmental dangers of preparing for war, which again focuses on several key areas of concern.

Part III discusses the future of warfare, examining the future of the United States and the things that need to change as technological advances continue. This look ahead covers the need to change ideas, attitudes, rules, and regulations. The reader will want to add personal speculations.

I wanted to provide readers with an overview of a massive problem rather than a textbook of the problems. I could have written volumes but purposely kept it simple and concise. Much of what is covered in the book is only an introduction to large and complex issues. For this reason, I have included an extensive appendix. Three appendices cover pertinent laws and treaties, addresses of resources for further information and assistance, and information and further reading divided by topics introduced throughout the book.

All across the country, Americans seem to be sending a message to the government. Tired of having no voice, citizens of the United States are beginning to take action. *The Ecology of War* provides a look back at what has happened so that Americans can understand what needs to be done in the future.

INTRODUCTION

SINCE THE ADVENT of people on Earth, humans have been changing their environment. Often the most notable changes are the results of warfare. During the 1991 Persian Gulf War, the world witnessed millions of gallons of oil pouring into the gulf waters. Television viewers around the world saw helpless birds and fish suffocate. Horror stories about the atrocities at the Kuwaiti Zoo flooded the airwaves. Scientists could only guess at the effects of hundreds of oil fires. Middle Eastern residents looked on helplessly as the midday skies turned black with smoke and an oily rain covered the country. Yet 1991 was not the first time, nor will it be the last time, that the environment has suffered at the hands of warring forces.

There are two overriding themes in the history of the United States military, and that of many other nations, up to and including the Persian Gulf War. Wartime strategy is tailored to the type of enemy being fought. The root of most environmental destruction is the aim—when the opponent is an agricultural society—to separate the people from their environment. This has played a big role in American policy, since a majority of America's wartime foes have been agricultural societies. Ever-increasing technological ability, especially in the twentieth century, has brought new ways to destroy the land, with more serious consequences. In early American history, technology was not advanced to the level that enabled long-term and devastating damage to the environment.

A second major driving force behind much military strategy is that the end always justifies the means. This became especially poignant in the Cold War years, when the "end" of containing the Soviet Union was justifiable at any cost. The domestic environment became an innocent victim, an easy sacrifice, in the fight against the "Evil Empire."

All of this played a key role in the Persian Gulf War, yet there was a marked deviation in the way that war was fought. The U.S. military found itself responding to new and different kinds of threats. Saddam Hussein's motives behind the environmental destruction during the Persian Gulf War were not the ones encountered in past wars. For the first time, accusations of environmental terrorism were leveled against a government and its leader. The environment itself was the direct target of the warfare—a threat held out openly to the world.

Even before Operation Desert Storm, however, environmental damage during warfare had been rapidly increasing in intensity over the past several decades. As technology became more advanced, efforts of warfare were more concentrated. People could be moved quickly, and immediate communication over long distances first became possible during the twentieth century. Humans began to learn to manipulate their environment to bring devastating results to an enemy.

Railroads initially played a major role in warfare during the American Civil War because they could move large numbers of troops quickly. Combined with more sophisticated weaponry, warfare took on a new tone. Destruction was more complete, devastation longer lasting.

Scorched-earth tactics were common during the Civil War. Scorched-earth methods are serious threats to the environment because they destroy the land completely. The most common method is fire. An accepted military practice is to scorch the land with massive fires, destroying crops, grasslands and pasture, and forests. The American South was largely an agrarian society, and the economic stability of the South depended on its agricultural lands. An entire way of life had been built up around that agricultural base. Using scorched-earth tactics proved to be a valuable military tool during the Civil War, specifically because of the agrarian South's dependence on the environment.

The most destructive campaigns of the Civil War were Sheridan's 1864 Shenandoah Valley campaign in Virginia and Sherman's march from Atlanta to Savannah, Georgia. Major General Philip Sheridan followed orders to destroy the land and all crops along the way in an attempt to starve the people of the South into submission. Sherman conducted his 1864 march through Georgia for similar purposes.

During the American Indian wars, the United States Army practiced several tactics of environmental damage. The army destroyed the Indians' food and crops and slaughtered entire bison herds on the plains. Each action was an attempt to starve out the Indians and force their surrender and submission.

During World War II, Hitler ordered the retreating German army to destroy the land before the Allies could take it. Nuclear detonations in Japan caused unprecedented environmental damage. The Vietnam War severely impacted the Vietnamese environment. American forces destroyed the forests used as hiding places for the mobile enemy forces, destroyed crops, and displaced local populations.

By the time the United States sent troops to the Persian Gulf, it was technologically possible to bring together hundreds of thousands of troops within a few weeks. The types of weapons used in the war are defined by advances in technology. Stealth fighters, undetectable by enemy radar, can deliver massive blows on the ground without any advance warning. Missiles guided by computer chips and "smart" bombs can hit targets with precision. Bigger and better airplanes deliver the most advanced bombs and missiles on an enemy far below—an enemy who remains anonymous and unseen by pilots thousands of feet overhead.

In the Persian Gulf War, in addition to the plundering

of Kuwait by invading Iraqi forces, much of Iraq—a struggling Third World country—was ravaged by the weapons of the Coalition Forces. The growing industrial base in Iraq made it strategically important for the military to destroy the Iraqi countryside as well as the cities. This situation of almost unlimited targets led to unprecedented environmental devastation, the effects of which will linger for years to come.

The environment nearly always suffers during war. Animal species become extinct. Forests become deserts or swamps. Jungles dry up. Fertile farmland becomes a mine field. Water becomes contaminated. Native vegetation disappears.

Despite these results, strangely enough, there is occasionally salvation in the midst of destruction. Some impacts are even positive. During World War II, the German submarine forces effectively shut down the North Atlantic fishing industry. Fish populations rose to an all-time high. "Off-limits" areas, such as the demilitarized zone between North and South Korea, often become wildlife sanctuaries.

The part the military establishment plays in this drama is interesting. Until after the Vietnam War, military planners did not give much thought to the environment. Environmental plans were aimed at lessening the environment's impact on the troops. The military often saw the environment as one more hardship to overcome on the battlefield. Many point to Vietnam, where dense jungles were another enemy for the forces to subdue, as one of the clearest examples ever of environmental damage during warfare.

Then, in August 1970, the deputy secretary of defense

gave the various services requirements outlining military compliance with the National Environmental Policy Act of 1969. The military has since become more aware of environmental concerns. In 1984, the Department of Defense (DoD) began the Defense Environmental Restoration Program (DERP). This program was designed to carry out the Installation Restoration Program (IRP) at military installations suspected of being contaminated. The IRP conducts tests to verify the reports. DERP also has a second focus, called Other Hazardous Waste (OHW) Operations. The OHW component of the program provides research, development, and demonstration programs designed to reduce the production of hazardous waste. Some critics would argue that the money spent on the program has been little more than an attempt at mollification.

In the annual report to Congress on the Defense Environmental Restoration Program in early 1990, then Deputy Assistant Secretary of Defense (Environment) William H. Parker III, stated that the department had "established environmental leadership as a top priority in DoD, not just in the evaluation and cleanup of our facilities, but throughout our operations." Parker went on to outline several key elements of the program designed to provide environmental awareness to each person within the department: DoD must effect cultural change to create an environmental ethic; compliance with environmental laws must be ensured and accountability made clear; people will be motivated and well trained in environmental issues; the appropriate amount of money must be budgeted to care for the environment; environmental training must be provided to every soldier, sailor, airman, marine, and civilian employee to clarify the environmental responsibilities to each person; communications and public affairs programs must be developed to foster environmental awareness; and regulatory relations between the Department of Defense and the environmental agencies must be improved.

Despite these moves and the changing policy, the environment's effect on the military usually remains a primary concern of military leaders. Military writing speaks of the laws that the Department of Defense must obey and of the public pressures to which the military commanders must respond. There is often talk in the military literature of the effect of the environment on the troops in battle and how troops should respond to and overcome environmental challenges.

Possible destruction of the environment during warfare is a threat to every human. Technology makes that fate even more complete and the possible consequences potentially more serious than ever before. By examining the impacts of war historically, perhaps it is possible to gain a better understanding of today's environmental concerns.

Americans and citizens of other nations around the world can no longer ignore the legacy the world's militaries have left. They are one of the leading causes of pollution. The Science for Peace Institute at the University of Toronto estimates that 10 to 30 percent of all environmental degradation in the world is a direct result of the various militaries. Defense activities can negatively impact land, air, wildlife, and water resources. A German report recently concluded that 6 to 10 percent of the world's air pollution is a result of the armed forces of the world—forces that are responsible for the emission of approximately two-thirds of all chlorofluorocarbon-113 released into the atmosphere. In the United States, the Department of Defense creates more than five times as much toxic waste as the five major U.S. chemical companies.

There is, however, much in the way of promise and of change in today's military. It is reassuring to learn that the real military—the men and women out doing the work—is made up of real people, not bureaucrats or politicians or warmongers. Yet there are still abuses and problems. There is a reluctance to admit that problems exist and to share problems with the public and let the people help solve them. Decades of military buildup and nonchalance provide a legacy gradually being made available for public scrutiny. It is time that the public look behind the scenes—Americans must take an interest in the military that was established to protect every citizen, to work *for* the public.

There is a solution. The ingenuity of the human race can reverse the damage that has been done. A first step is to understand the problems, to look deeper and to reflect on the entire history of our country and our military. That is the object of this book: to help individuals understand, reflect, and form new ideas about a concern for the environment during warfare.

PART ONE

EARLY
HISTORY
OF
WARFARE

The environment has always been a victim in warfare. Two major sources of environmental degradation can be referred to again and again—the incidental results of weapons and maneuvers, and the direct results of attempting to deny resources to the enemy. This is the repeating pattern, and even ancient stories relate some of the disasters.

Two of the earliest recorded instances of a direct attack on the environment are in the Bible. Judges 15:4–5 relates the story of Samson and the Philistines and tells of yet another form of direct environmental destruction. Samson burned corn crops, vineyards, and olive trees belonging to the Philistines.

Judges 9:45 recounts the story of Abimelech conquering Schechem. Upon entering the city and killing all the people, Abimelech sowed the ground with salt to make it infertile.

The tactic of sowing the soil with salt also was undertaken during the Third Punic War, when Rome captured Carthage sometime around 150 B.C. The attacks on the environment eventually became more severe as technology advanced.

Even the use of deadly gases, which became widespread in modern warfare during World War I, has been utilized throughout history. As early as 2000 B.C. chemicals were used in ancient India, where various incendiary devices were designed to give off smoke and toxic fumes.

During the Peloponnesian War, in 429 B.C., King Archidamus led the Peloponnesians against the town of Plataea. He began his attack by cutting down all the fruit trees around the town to form a palisade. After more than two months of trying to collapse the city walls by piling dirt, rocks, and even more chopped trees against them, Archidamus turned to fire, and he combined it with the use of chemicals to create a deadly weapon. Wood covered with sulfur and pitch was set afire and thrown over the walls. According to Thucydides' account of the burning, it was a fire unlike any ever set by human beings. Luckily for the Plataeans, nature fought back. A great rainstorm put out the fire and saved the city.

In 674, the Byzantines used chemical warfare to end a seven-year siege on Constantinople by Muslims. A flammable mixture of sulfur, niter, and naphtha was loaded into flame throwers and used against Arab ships. The

"Greek Fire" terrified the Muslim troops, destroyed many of their ships, and ended the stalemate at Constantinople.

Frequently war-besieged nations ravaged their own environment, attempting to turn back the enemy or to leave no resources behind for the conquerors. Incidents of self-inflicted damage, such as scorched-earth tactics, are common throughout history.

In 480 B.C., Pericles directed the Athenians to withdraw to save themselves from an advancing enemy and suggested that they destroy their land as they retreated.

In the early 1200s, during Mongol invasions of Asia and eastern Europe under Genghis Khan, all livestock and crops not taken by the enemy were ravaged. One of the most ruinous acts was the destruction of the irrigation works near Baghdad. A two-thousand-year-old irrigation system on the Tigris River had been supplying water to one of the most highly developed areas of the world. Direct attack on the irrigation system effectively toppled an entire civilization. Genghis Khan went on to conquer Baghdad and completely wasted the city.

Biological warfare is also documented in medieval history. In the 1300s, Kaffa was a major port on the Black Sea. For more than three years, the city withstood an invasion attempt by the Mongol Tartars, until biological warfare was used in 1346. The Mongols catapulted the bodies of people who had died from the plague over the walls of the city. The resulting epidemic in Kaffa became its downfall. The few survivors among the Genoese who were defending the walled city eventually fled to Italy and took the "black death" with them.

All of these actions showed a tremendous understanding of the long-term effects of such activities on the environment. Prior to the Industrial Revolution, people were dependent on the land. Destroying it was guaranteed to subdue an enemy. There were tactics carefully planned to this end, and these strategies are still pursued today for the same reasons, particularly in societies dependent on an agricultural base, such as Third World countries.

Although the causes of environmental damage during warfare have remained largely the same throughout history, the consequences are changing in modern times. Large populations and advanced technology have made environmental damage even more catastrophic. The magnitude of modern weapons has changed. Greater destruction is now possible in a single day than in months of warfare two thousand years ago—even if nuclear weapons are not used. Another change is air power. Not only has the capability of aircraft to deliver bombs and troops to distant targets changed but so too has the bird's-eye view airplanes have during combat. From the seat of the cockpit, a pilot can see the battlefield from above, picking out the hiding places, the strengths, and the weaknesses of the enemy. Yet pilots cannot see inside thick forests in areas where trees obscure their vision from the air. This trend has turned trees into an "enemy" on the battlefield. Prior to air power, forest destruction was either incidental to warfare or part of a scorched-earth tactic. Today, forests have become specific military targets for armies.

Given the long human history of direct environmental damage during war, it seems unlikely that the tendency will completely disappear in the future. Attention also should be focused on what happens following warfare and during preparations for war, as modern military technologies and philosophies have increased the potential for environmental degradation before and after battle. Military history can be used as a measure of current and future military-related environmental devastation and possible long-term effects.

PART TWO

MODERN WARFARE

1.

ENVIRONMENTAL DAMAGE
DURING WAR

FEW DISASTERS come close to the environmental damage caused by modern warfare. There are three basic types of damage done to the environment during warfare. The first two categories have been observed throughout history. Most obvious is *direct destruction* of the environment: intentional damage to achieve a specific military objective, such as burning fields and orchards to starve out the enemy or defoliating jungles to reveal the enemy's hiding places. *Incidental direct destruction* is caused by deliberate acts that have some other tactical purpose, such as digging trenches and bombing supply lines.

The remaining category, while often less obvious during the battle and only examined in recent years, may have even greater long-term effects on the environment. *Indirect destruction* is usually the hardest to foresee and the effect most often overlooked. An example of indirect destruction is when birds become extinct because their habitat was destroyed by fighting.

Colonel Ken Cornelius, an air force officer on the staff of the assistant secretary of defense for the environment, confirms the extent of the damage and how the role of the military often comes into conflict with the environment. "If we're going to break things and kill people, and that's what war's about, if push comes to shove, that's what we're there to do. I can't think of too much that's more damaging to the environment than war."

AMERICAN PATTERNS

There seem to be few long-term environmental effects from the American Revolution. However, identifying such damage is problematic because there were few direct reports of the events. Perhaps it was a matter of the military leaders not understanding the relevance of the problem. Given the fact that warfare throughout history has involved some degree of environmental damage, it seems likely that there were indeed some instances of environmental degradation. It also seems likely, based on historical evidence, that humans were aware of at least some of the impacts of their actions on the environment, at least in the ways in which those actions affected human survival.

The more likely scenario is that the colonists felt

inclined to minimize damage to the American land. Many of those involved in the Revolution were landowners with a personal interest in reducing environmental attacks, for monetary reasons rather than some intrinsic understanding of the stress on the environment itself. If the war had been fought on British soil, or if the British had not felt some sense of ownership and kinship with the colonies, the results might have been different.

Tactics of environmental destruction were used frequently on Indian lands and in areas known at that time as the frontier. Native American societies, especially those in the Eastern United States, were largely agrarian and depended on the environment for their survival.

During the American Revolution, General George Washington directed the colonists, under General John Sullivan, to destroy the environment to defeat the Indians fighting on behalf of the British. In the fall of 1779, the colonists razed the entire corn crop about to be harvested by the Iroquois Nation in New York. In addition to the crops, fruit orchards were cut down. Evidence shows that most of the Indians fled before Sullivan's army could get close, resulting in few human deaths. However, Sullivan basically destroyed the agricultural economy and the homeland of the Iroquois Nation. The colonists hoped that the Indians would eventually die during the harsh winter with no food or resources. The military, although loosely organized at the time of the Revolution, began the American tradition of environmental warfare. The final end justified the often extreme methods of achieving those objectives.

As American expansion moved west, the Indian Wars

also moved west. During the Navajo Wars in Arizona in the early 1860s, the United States Army systematically destroyed the Navajos' corn crops, various orchards, and all of their sheep and other livestock.

In 1865, General Philip Sheridan became commander of the Department of the West. Upon taking over command, General Sheridan ordered the annihilation of the remaining bison herds on the plains. Understanding the importance of the bison to Indian culture, Sheridan predicted that their elimination would lead to the ultimate destruction of the Indian populations throughout the Plains states. Tribes in this region did indeed come close to starvation as the bison herds disappeared. Once plentiful in America, the bison became a nearly extinct symbol of a bygone era, a direct result of intentional military policy.

These tactics utilized during the later years of the Indian Wars were not new. In fact, the two prominent figures of the Indian Wars—Sheridan as commander of the Department of the West and General William Tecumseh Sherman as General Grant's Chief of Staff—became expert in such methods during the American Civil War.

THE AMERICAN CIVIL WAR

The developing American military utilized whatever strategies were necessary to separate the enemy from their means of survival. Numerous instances of environmental devastation occurred during the Civil War. Sherman's march through Georgia and Sheridan's campaign in Virginia's Shenandoah Valley both involved acts of deliberate environmental destruction.

The concept that became known as "total war" was developed by Karl von Clausewitz in the 1830s. Total war was first utilized during the Civil War years, and involved the destruction of crops, food, and actual property. In an 1863 report to General Grant, General Sherman indicated that the land had been so wasted that it could no longer support human life. Sustenance had to be carried into areas where Sherman's army had been. In Georgia alone, it has been estimated that Sherman's troops destroyed close to 10 million acres of land. All crops and livestock between Atlanta and Savannah were either confiscated or destroyed.

Virginia's Shenandoah Valley was one of the areas hardest hit during the American Civil War. Sheridan's Shenandoah Valley campaign of 1864 caused massive destruction. In a personal letter to General Sheridan at the beginning of this campaign, General Grant ordered Sheridan to turn the valley into a barren wasteland, "so that crows flying over it for the balance of this season will have to carry their provender with them." Sheridan responded with a promise to Grant that when his troops were finished, there would be little left "for man or beast."

General Grant also made his plans for the valley known to several of the generals serving under Sheridan. In an August 1864 letter to Major General Hunter, Grant instructed Hunter: "It is desirable that nothing should be left to invite the enemy to return. Take all provisions, forage and Stock wanted for the use of your Command. Such as cannot be consumed destroy. . . . The people should be informed that so long as an Army can subsist among them, recurrences of these raids must be expected."

Along the length of the valley, fires scorched the agriculturally rich region and left the people begging for mercy. Historians have long studied these campaigns to understand why the leaders chose such destructive tactics and why they were aimed primarily at the land the civilians depended on for survival. In his Report of Operations of the Cavalry Corps in 1864, Sheridan specifically stated the reason for scorched-earth warfare. "These men and women did not care how many were killed or maimed, so long as war did not come to their doors, but as soon as it did come in the shape of loss of property, they earnestly prayed for its termination." Sheridan believed that the war would end sooner if the civilians felt its impact. "Total war" was used to break the will of the civilian population in the South, just as it had been used against Native American populations and would be used again on the western frontier in the coming years.

Numerous other attacks on the environment occurred throughout the Civil War. When Sherman's army moved across Mississippi in 1863, there was an estimated $4 million (in 1863 dollar values) in losses resulting from intentional damage to all the natural resources that might have been beneficial to the South.

In addition to the direct destruction of the environment, there is an enormous amount of incidental and indirect environmental damage done during any kind of warfare. The Civil War was a long, harsh war, and nature frequently got in the way. Journalist and Civil War soldier Ambrose Bierce vividly described harm to the land in his essays on the battles of the Civil War. He wrote of trees that were only splinters protruding from the ground after a battle and other trees that remained standing but were completely riddled, up to a height of about twenty feet, with bullet and shrapnel holes. In fact, in one essay he describes his surprise at finding a forest with no scarred trees, with underbrush still intact, and with soil not trampled. He knew instantly that no battle had been fought there and no army had ever camped there.

One of the most ruinous environmental tragedies of the Civil War occurred during the Battle of the Wilderness in Virginia. This area was a dense forest, and Confederate troops, lying in wait for Union troops, had used trees, bushes, and other forest material to construct breastworks to hide behind. As fighting broke out in the dry, brittle forest, sparks from the soldiers' guns ignited the dead leaves and dry trees. The fire quickly spread to the stacked brush and limbs of the hastily built breastworks and soon engulfed huge sections of forest.

Accidental fires are not unusual during war. In the eastern United States, where forests grew fast and thick, fire damage during the Civil War was particularly devastating. In the Battle of the Wilderness, breastworks added to the fire's ferocity; at Shiloh, decaying foliage lying on the ground became a tinderbox. Thick foliage from the previous summer had fallen and dried out, and sparks from guns set off the dry tinder during the early spring battle. Ambrose Bierce describes how he walked through ankle-deep ash left by a forest fire following the battle of Shiloh.

The breastworks at the Battle of the Wilderness were

hastily constructed, resulting in fire. Often breastworks were elaborate and included a massive system of trenches, and these left a different kind of mark on the forest. One example was the Bentonville Battlefield in North Carolina. There, a series of embattlements and trenches were constructed. In fact, over one hundred years later, it is still possible to pick out the trench line—for in the midst of a dense hardwood forest in North Carolina, a thin line without vegetation clearly marks where a trench once ran.

American warfare during the half-century between the end of the Civil War and the entrance of the United States into World War I remained much the same. Methods similar to those already described were used in Haiti, Nicaragua, and the Philippines, which the U.S. took under its sphere of influence during those years of expansion.

One of General Arthur MacArthur's favorite policies during the Philippines campaign in 1900 was reconcentration. An estimated 10,000 locals were "reconcentrated" into protective zones. The outlying areas, including all crops, livestock, and buildings, were then destroyed to deny sustenance to the guerrillas. MacArthur drew on past practices, specifically those of the American Civil War, and surmised that without the food of the surrounding countryside, the guerrillas would have to give up the fight.

Then came the "big one," the "war to end all wars."

WORLD WAR I

World War I marked a turning point in modern warfare. Troops could quickly travel long distances. Bombs could destroy an enemy never seen face-to-face. Aerial warfare and tanks changed the way people fought and died.

The most extensive environmental damage during World War I was in France. In the Battle of the Somme, French countryside was destroyed. Trenches cut across farmland, leaving infertile areas still visible today. In her book about the Somme, Lyn MacDonald interviewed soldiers who commented on the devastation to the French farmlands. One area, Thiepval Ridge, was described by the soldiers as completely barren, with no grass, trees, or animals left alive. After twenty-four hours of battle, the lush High Wood was destroyed: trees were reduced to splinters, trunks were uprooted, the whole area was transformed into a death scene. Close to 250,000 acres of farmland were devastated so severely that it was determined the area could no longer serve any agricultural purpose. The land was instead planted with trees.

Generally, the most extensive damage of World War I was sustained by forests, and again France was the hardest hit. During the war, 1.5 million acres of forest land in France were in occupied zones and battle zones. An estimated 494,000 acres of French forests were leveled and had to be replanted after the war. In addition to battle damage, an enormous amount of lumber—some 20 billion board feet—was harvested for the war effort, most of it by the Allies. With the onslaught of World War II, barely twenty years later, the forests had little chance for recovery.

Animal populations were also severely impacted by the widespread fighting during World War I. European buffalo, or wisent, were endangered prior to the start of the war and had already been reduced to a small population in eastern Europe. The wisent's habitat was virtually destroyed by the German occupation forces, who cut down the Polish forest to obtain lumber needed for military operations. With no place left to hide, the wisent was easy prey for the hungry German forces. Fortunately, zoologists have been able to increase the herds' numbers once again.

An often overlooked casualty of World War I was the destruction to agricultural lands in the United States. In the 1939 book *America Begins Again*, Katherine Glover contends that the war did more to devastate the soils in the United States than anything in the nation's history prior to that time. She argues that the battlefields "spread to the cotton fields of the South, the cornfields of the Middle West, and the wheat fields of the Great Plains." Ms. Glover describes the posters displayed across the country during the war that declared, "Food will win the war," reflecting the nation's attitudes. While Europe fought the battles on their land, the United States grew the food needed to feed the Allied world.

During the World War I years, 40 million new acres of land were cultivated. Land that was not fit for growing crops was nevertheless forced into production. Natural reservoirs and wetlands were destroyed in the Northwest to make room for wheat crops. Native grasses were plowed under in the Southwest to create new wheat farms—farms that were eventually overtaken by drought and eroded by the wind. Cotton was overplanted in the South, depleting the soil of nutrients. Timber forests in Minnesota, Wisconsin, and Michigan were destroyed to meet wartime needs.

In indirect ways, even some animal populations in the United States were impacted by World War I. During the Theodore Roosevelt administration of 1901 through 1909, there was grave concern over the plight of birds in the United States. The bird populations were decreasing dramatically as a result of the loss of wetlands and unchecked hunting. Roosevelt's secretary of state was able to get legislation passed that enabled the president to negotiate international treaties protecting the migration of birds. With the onset of World War I, the treaty negotiations came to a halt. Throughout the war, bird populations continued to decrease at unprecedented rates. The treaty was not ratified by the United States and Great Britain (on behalf of Canada) until 1916 because of World War I.

COUNTERINSURGENCY IN THE YEARS BETWEEN THE WORLD WARS

Following World War I, the sentiment grew that technology could indeed assist armies in winning wars. Transportation was rapidly improving, and Americans found themselves in far-off places, fighting "little" wars in Nicaragua and Haiti, for example.

The United States Marine Corps participated in most of the conflicts between the two world wars. Aircraft were used in Nicaragua and Haiti, both for reconnaissance and to drop bombs. When the radio became widely available in 1921, the airplane became a more important weapon.

In 1927, Americans dropped seventeen-pound fragmentation bombs on Nicaragua during attempts to stop the civil war there. The real success of the airplane, however, did not come until late 1927 and early 1928. U.S. forces had only twelve planes available for use in the area. Despite that small number, for one year beginning in mid-1927, the United States Marines carried out eighty-four attacks on guerrilla strongholds. A total of 300 bombs and 30,000 rounds of ammunition were fired from the aircraft at the guerrilla forces in Nicaragua. While environmental damage from these attacks was not extensive, it set a precedent for the future use of air power by the U.S. military. These same tactics—bombing the ground and destroying vegetation to oust guerrilla forces—defined the strategy of the Vietnam War.

Another method used to counter insurgents was called "reconnaissance by fire." It required troops to approach possible ambush spots shooting. The area was torn apart with firepower from submachine guns before it was actually entered.

Counterinsurgency was quickly becoming a favorite way of fighting for the United States Marine Corps. Then Adolf Hitler began invading the countries of Europe and tactics changed once again.

WORLD WAR II

As we have seen, scorched-earth tactics have been used repeatedly throughout both ancient and modern history.

At times it has been for a purpose similar to the one in the American Civil War or the Indian Wars: destroy the enemy's land and means of sustenance and eventually the enemy will submit. At other times, however, it has been for very different reasons. As in the example of Pericles and the Athenians during the Peloponnesian War, scorched-earth policies sometimes arise out of the decision to leave nothing behind for the conquering armies. This often proved to be the case during World War II.

In World War II, the Germans occupied Norway from 1940 to 1945. Initial environmental damage was done by the Norwegians themselves as a means of defense against the German aggressors. During the night of November 25 and 26, 1940, the locals in western Norway caused landslides throughout the country. Heavy rains and snowfall in the mountains made the land soft. Norwegians placed several small charges of dynamite, triggering landslides. This made it difficult for the Germans to advance, since rocks, brush, and trees blocked the roads.

As the war continued, the Germans became fearful of their position in Norway, expecting a Soviet attack. To destroy everything of value to the Allies, the German army retreated and destroyed everything in an area close to 15 million acres. Property, crops, and forests were demolished, along with wildlife in the area. The reindeer population of 95,000 was reduced by half during that period. Following the war, the local environment gradually seemed to heal, and the reindeer population had increased to 90,000 only fifteen years after the end of World War II. Long-term effects were never studied in the area.

Another area severely affected by the German army

was the Netherlands. As the German army advanced toward their country, the people of the Netherlands fought hard to defend themselves. In this country of dikes and canals, it was a temporary fix when the Dutch opened irrigation gates in the main waterline running through the country. This had been done earlier in Dutch history with success. In 1672, Louis XIV, king of France, declared war on Holland. As the French army marched into the country, William of Orange ordered the dikes opened, flooding the land with saltwater that eventually turned back the aggressors. The plan was not as successful against Hitler's German army—flooding was shallow and only temporarily slowed down the German advance. The Germans were finally able to break through into the Netherlands. In an attempt to starve out and subdue the enemy, the Germans also sacrificed the environment, ruining an estimated 17 percent of the productive farmland by flooding the area with saltwater.

The Germans were not the only ones to use water as an offensive weapon during World War II. In May 1943, the Allies bombed two large dams in the Ruhr Valley in Germany in an attempt to destroy Germany's industrial economic base and to make it impossible for Hitler to produce any additional equipment. Destruction of the dams released an enormous amount of water—an estimated 34.3 billion gallons of water from the Möhne Dam and another 52.8 billion gallons from the Eder Dam—resulting in the deaths of over 6,500 cattle and pigs and the destruction of nearly 7,500 acres of agricultural land.

Even in the continental United States there was small-scale environmental damage during World War II. Japanese submarines fired gasoline and oil bombs into the forests in the Pacific Northwest. While the bombs had little environmental effect in the United States, similar bombs proved detrimental to the Chinese environment. Bombs destroyed dams on the Yellow River, flooding huge sections of the country.

Some of the heaviest destruction during World War II occurred as a result of bombing and shelling. During the occupation of France throughout the war, France's forests again suffered badly. Direct actions of war are estimated to have destroyed nearly 1 million acres of forest in France. Forest fires devastated another 247,000 acres of forest, and indirect damage such as shrapnel and erosion from clearing large land areas caused additional losses.

The unique ecosystems involved in warfare during World War II brought several unique environmental problems. Warfare in the deserts of North Africa and on islands in the South Pacific was especially detrimental.

The desert surface was damaged by tanks and other military vehicles, along with bombing and shelling activities. Vegetation that was growing in the harsh climate was destroyed; dust storms became much more frequent. A study from 1945 to 1946 found that dust storms occurred in greater frequency in areas of military activity. It was discovered that in areas where the soil surface had been disturbed, it took only half the wind velocity normally needed to bring about a dust storm.

Islands in the South Pacific were often victims of widespread environmental degradation during World War II. The islands, mostly small and isolated, had fragile and closely interconnected ecosystems that were easily knocked off-balance by warfare. The American military utilized similar tactics on each island throughout the war in the Pacific. A first step was to blockade the island with naval power and bombard the island from the air and the sea for an extended period. Once the enemy positions had been weakened, the U.S. military would cross the coral reefs with landing vehicles and tanks to land on the beaches. Once on the island, the Americans used flame throwers, tanks, bulldozers, and any other means available at the time to clear the land. After the enemy had been subdued, the natural resources of the island were exploited for military purposes.

Battle tales from Corregidor include vivid images of shell-shattered trees, enormous grass fires, and visibility blocked by smoke and blowing dust in a land that was once a green jungle. W. Robert Moore, a Pacific correspondent for the National Geographic Society in 1945, wrote numerous articles while he traveled with American troops in the South Pacific. He comments in many of the articles that he never had to ask which islands had seen fighting; the devastated landscapes made it obvious. Fighting on the tiny island of Peleliu was unusually tough. The Japanese army had hidden in the thick jungle there for quite some time. At the end of the battle, very few of the trees were left with no battle scars. Even large trees were split from exploding shells. In addition to uprooted trees, destroyed vegetation, and rapid erosion, craters caused by falling and exploding bombs gave large areas a pockmarked appearance.

Another disastrous consequence of the war in the Pacific was the destruction of the coral reefs. When troops landed on a new island, one of the first orders of business was to build a runway. Bulldozers were brought in to level the land and uproot any remaining trees. The topsoil was then scraped off with the aid of large scrapers pulled by tractors. In isolated island areas, the most readily available source of material for runways was coral. Loads of coral were brought to the cleared areas by the large tractors. Coral rock was mined in open pits. In one of his *National Geographic* articles, Moore reported that an entire mountainside on Saipan was torn open to provide coral rock to the American troops. The coral was then crushed and compacted to make a runway.

Engineers preferred live coral, however, if it was available. Live coral was collected below the waterline by bulldozers and then crushed into a base for runways. In addition to deliberately digging up the living coral reefs for runways, reefs were damaged by tanks and amtracs (amphibious tractors) running over them. Many of the islands were completely surrounded by coral reefs. To provide access to the island and to enable the LSTs (a type of landing ship; the official military term is Landing Ship, Tank) to reach the shore, tanks and amphibious craft were driven over the reefs to crush the coral and provide access to the beach. The coral was completely devastated in some areas of the South Pacific, and there are still areas today where the coral has never recovered.

As a result of such severe costs to the habitat, wildlife in the South Pacific was severely impacted during World War II. Of particular significance was the damage done to the bird populations. Nesting places were destroyed. Patterns of migration were interrupted. Birds were killed and eggs smashed by the thousands. Nonindigenous predators were introduced onto the islands, such as dogs, cats, and rats.

Numerous bird species were killed off during World War II. In many cases, rats brought onto the islands were the direct cause of extinction. The largest single cause of extinction was elimination of habitat. The Laysan rail and Laysan finch were confirmed completely wiped out during World War II as a result of a rat infestation brought by the troops and destruction of habitat. Other birds have shared a similar fate due to bombing, rats, and military presence in traditional nesting areas. Some of the species to suffer this end include the Wake Island rail, the Marianas mallard, the Marianas megapode, and the brown booby.

There were other reported accidental killings of animals throughout World War II. It has been reported, although actual statistics were not assembled, that a large number of whales were killed during the war. Whales were evidently mistaken for submarines by gunners. Marine life was also endangered during World War II by oil spills, usually resulting from the bombing and sinking of oil tankers—an estimated 300 during the course of World War II.

Oceans were also threatened from the release of chemical agents during World War II. In late 1943, the Germans bombed Allied ships anchored at Bari harbor in Italy. One of the ships attacked was carrying 220,500 pounds of mustard gas bombs. Upon impact and the sinking of the ship, large quantities of mustard gas were leaked into the Adriatic Sea. Unfortunately for the local residents, the gas sank to the bottom of the harbor rather than completely dissipating in the water. Mustard gas lying at the bottom of a body of water is toxic to mammals and humans, and exists as a serious threat for many years. According to Swedish experts, the released mustard gas forms a protective layer underwater. The protective layer helps the chemical agent retain its effectiveness for many years. In addition to the mustard gas itself, the by-products created as the mustard gas breaks down are also toxic to humans, animals, and fish, and scientists estimate that some of the by-products will remain dangerous for as long as 400 years.

One of the most devastating and perhaps longest-lasting of the effects of World War II on the environment was the detonation of nuclear bombs over Hiroshima and Nagasaki, Japan. There were two nuclear bombs dropped on Japan during World War II, only three days apart, in August 1945. In addition to the immediate damage from the bombs upon impact, there was further damage caused by massive fires, "black rain" that fell over a period of several days, radiation in the soil and water for long periods of time, and plant and animal life destroyed, injured, or mutated by the explosions and the resulting radiation.

Following the blast in Hiroshima, a fireball swept through the city, burning for as long as six hours. Fires were accompanied by massive rains that washed away much of the soil, already loosened by elimination of the vegetation.

Following World War II and its ferocity, Americans believed that war could never get much worse. Then American warfare entered a new era. The Cold War began.

Fighting began halfway around the world in places most Americans had never heard of—Korea and Vietnam.

KOREA AND VIETNAM

One of the favorite American strategies in Korea was the bombing of North Korea's irrigation dams. The bombings destroyed the dams, released North Korea's agricultural water supply, and disrupted the supply of rice to the local citizens. The United States military relied heavily on the age-old tactic of destroying the country's food supply and economic base. Korea was an agrarian society dependent on the land, so that land became a military target of the war.

Scorched-earth warfare took on new dimensions in Asia, especially during the Vietnam War. Under the broad term of *defoliation,* officially carried out to deprive the enemy of the lush jungle cover, machinery and chemicals were utilized to destroy crops and water supplies as well, in an aim to subdue the people and starve out the enemy.

The use of chemicals has been the most publicized method of defoliation. Operation Ranch Hand was the most infamous of the U.S. government's spraying operations. Herbicides were used in Southeast Asia beginning in the early 1960s, peaked between 1967 and 1969, and stopped during 1971. According to an Agent Orange Brief published in 1991 by the Department of Veterans Affairs, over 20 million gallons of herbicides were employed on more than 6 million acres of land in Southeast Asia.

Of all herbicides used, 75 percent of the total was focused on the forests of our ally in the Vietnam War, South Vietnam. Areas with repeated sprayings, which occurred on more than 65 percent of the sprayed land in Vietnam, showed considerably more immediate damage to the vegetation than areas sprayed only once. The fragile jungle ecosystem is much more complex than the visible effects on trees and plants, however. The continued survival of Vietnam's forests depends on animals, birds, insects, and the water supply—the interplay of a jungle ecosystem. Soil in the region does not hold nutrients for long periods. Without the normal vegetation, areas can quickly become depleted and erosion of the soil will occur.

Mangrove forests, a vital part of the tropical ecosystem, were decimated in the Vietnam War. Mangrove trees grow only in the world's tropics, along tropical and semitropical coastlines and are periodically covered with salt water. The trees play a unique role in the fragile wet environment of the tropics. Large, above-ground roots extend from the trunks to the ground; these roots add support to the trees as they grow in the wet ground, in saltwater estuaries, and on riverbanks. The roots create a tangled thicket within mangrove forests that catch the debris and hold the sedimentary soil in place along the riverbank. This thicket often provided a hiding place for snipers attempting to disrupt river traffic, as well as cover for Vietnamese troops hiding from American aircraft.

Absence of the mangroves along riverbanks leads to erosion and a gradual wearing away of the shoreline. The mangrove has its own built-in filtering system to enable the trees to feed from saltwater. The salt is filtered out by the roots, sending only pure water to the leaves. Decaying leaves along the riverbanks further help the ecosystem by providing nutrients to a variety of species, such as fish and crabs.

It has been estimated that more than 300,000 acres of mangrove forests were lost through use of defoliants and napalm during the Vietnam War, severely stressing the area's mangrove ecosystem. Even today, nearly 20 percent of the tidal mangroves and 30 percent of the rear or upriver mangroves have not recovered. Areas of wasteland have been named "Agent Orange Museums" by the local residents.

Operation Ranch Hand, officially called Operation Hades, was not aimed solely at the forests. In addition to damage done to jungles to reduce cover available to the enemy, crops were also sprayed. Following a long tradition of crop destruction aimed at breaking the will of the people, the military often deliberately ravaged farmland, crops, stores of harvested crops, garden plots, and fruit trees. This tactic was intended to undermine any sympathy and support that may have existed among the civilian population, especially in the South, for the guerrillas and the North Vietnamese. The attitude of the military toward Operation Ranch Hand can best be judged by their unofficial motto, "Only We Can Prevent Forests."

Despite the horror of chemical defoliation and its lasting presence in the soil and water supplies, some of the worst environmental damage occurred as a result of Rome plows. A Rome plow is an 11-foot-wide, 2.5-ton blade fitted with a 3-foot splitting lance attached to the front of a 20-ton tractor. The Rome plow operators dubbed themselves Rome Runners and Jungle Eaters, symbolic of the damage they could do.

Rome plows were used to clear massive amounts of land for various purposes—for runways or new military bases or to deny jungle cover to the enemy. These huge tractors could each clear one acre of land per hour, and more than 150 tractors operated daily. Estimates were that over 1,000 acres of land were cleared daily by the tractors in South Vietnam.

This type of massive land clearing had never before been technologically possible. In addition to the damage to trees and vegetation, the Rome plows brought about severe erosion and destruction of animal life and habitat. Because of erosion, damage by floods on the unprotected land became a severe threat in Vietnam.

Attempts were also made to use forest fire as a weapon. According to a U.S. Forest Service Report declassified in 1983, the Joint Chiefs of Staff had requested in late 1965 that a program be developed to "determine the feasibility of dehydrating jungle growth to the point where such material would support combustion, and to initiate development of operational means for determining the specific conditions under which there is the greatest probability of destroying jungle or forest growth by fire."

In December 1965, the Advanced Research Projects Agency began work on ARPA Order 818 in conjunction with the Division of Fire and Atmospheric Sciences Research of the U.S. Forest Service. To carry out the order, the Forest Service initiated three full-scale operational tests in Vietnam from January through April 1967. It was discovered that areas already treated with defoliants burned better than green areas. One of the most successful uses of fire as a weapon in Vietnam was a large fire in the U Minh area, in Southwest Vietnam. The original U Minh fire was not started by American forces. However, a second fire was started by the Americans in an adjacent area, and the entire U Minh fire was then assisted by the American forces and closely studied by the advisory group.

The estimate of final effects of the U Minh forest fire was submitted as part of the ARPA report entitled "Forest Fire as a Military Weapon":

- 75 to 85 percent of the true forest destroyed
- 50 percent of various outlying swamps destroyed
- Hundreds of tons of ammunition, rice, and petroleum products destroyed
- 100 to 200 Viet Cong killed or incapacitated while either fighting the fire or by rockets and air strikes in the area
- The probable dislocation of large quantities of supplies and ammunition and the relocation of several major Viet Cong headquarters and rear service areas
- The increased opportunity for aerial reconnaissance of the area
- The lack of lumber and possible food shortage for the local populace
- The increased danger of floods in areas adjacent to the forest since there are no longer trees or underbrush to provide watershed

Fire continued to be utilized as a weapon during the Vietnam War, although with mixed results. One of the most successful experiments was in the Plain of Reeds. The Plain of Reeds is the largest submerged area in all of Vietnam, covering nearly 2 million acres in the Mekong Delta. These wetlands were home to hundreds of thousands of birds such as cormorants, egrets, herons, ducks, storks, and cranes, and a variety of wetland grasses, lotuses, and water lilies. Large freshwater tarpon also found homes in the region. Wild mammals lived in the vast wetlands, among them numerous species endangered elsewhere—including tapir, kouprey, a species of bear, and the gibbon.

The area was also covered with mighty cajeput trees, reaching up to 60 feet tall at times. Floating rice was abundant and provided a vital source of food to the rural populations.

The American military discovered that by digging canals through the Plain of Reeds, the mangrove marshlands could be dried out during the dry season. This practice made the upper eight inches of soil barren and useless. Sulfur then rose to the surface of the dry soil, creating sulfuric acid. No longer could the Plain of Reeds support fish, floating rice, or the bird and other wildlife populations. The Americans soon discovered that the dry areas, normally too wet to burn, became easy targets for fires. Napalm was used to destroy the cajeput forests. A vital and major ecosystem in Vietnam was laid waste by the war.

In addition to new technology introduced in Southeast Asia, the American military relied heavily on more conventional warfare, such as aerial bombings. The sheer force of the bombing, however, took an unprecedented toll on the environment. Between 1965 and 1970 alone, more than double the amount of munitions was used in Vietnam than in Europe and the Pacific during all of World War II. It has been estimated that close to 16 million tons of munitions, including aerial munitions, ground munitions, and naval munitions, were utilized by the U.S. military in Southeast Asia.

Craters left by these bombs are still evident today throughout Vietnam. In a series of studies conducted by Arthur Westing between 1969 and 1973, Westing estimated that there were more than 30 million explosions in Southeast Asia, and each left a crater. The craters, averaging 30 feet in diameter and containing no topsoil, have turned much of Vietnam's lush landscape into something that resembles the moon. The entire ecosystem has been affected, and many areas are infertile. Even today, some twenty years after the fighting, many of the craters remain filled with water, creating drainage problems, providing a habitat for numerous disease-bearing organisms, and making land difficult or impossible to cultivate.

Other environmental effects of bombing resulted from the large amount of flying metal, or shrapnel, which killed any wildlife and trees that happened to be in its path. It has been estimated that shrapnel often extended out more than 300 feet in all directions from a blast site.

One especially poignant story of the bombing in Vietnam came from an Air Force B-52 pilot, now a colonel still on active military duty. The pilot generally participated only in nighttime bombing raids. Instructed where to drop bombs, pilots were also given an alternative location in case something happened and bombs could not be dropped at the chosen location. The alternative location was always the same spot along the Ho Chi Minh Trail. One evening, there was a full moon as this pilot dropped his bomb load at the alternative location. As he banked and came back over the drop area, the landscape below him was visible in the moonlight. The Vietnamese landscape, according to this pilot's account, appeared identical to photographs he had seen of the moon. No life was visible below him, only craters for as far as he could see toward the horizon. The pilot realized the full impact of what he was doing at that precise moment. He had always thought of the missions as just another day on the job until that night when he realized the complete devastation being brought to the country and its people. He said he never felt the same way about his missions in Vietnam again after that night.

Wildlife in Southeast Asia was greatly impacted by the war. In addition to the loss of habitat caused by bombs, defoliants, land clearing, and fires, as mentioned above, animals caught in the cross fire were frequent casualties during the decades of war. There are eleven rare species of mammals found only in Southeast Asia. Of those eleven species, four are now in danger of extinction. Several other species, though not unique to the area, are threatened. The red-shanked douc langur, a small monkey, is one of the species not found anywhere else in the world, and is threatened. In addition, the pileated gibbon, Owston's civet, and the kouprey are all endangered in their last remaining habitat in the world.

Some of the larger species of wild animals were able to partially escape the war. While populations of muntjacs and other type of deer, gaurs and other wild cattle, bantengs, wild pigs, elephants, and tigers became nearly extinct in South Vietnam, they thrived in eastern Cambodia, away from the dangers of war. In fact, there were reports late in the war of a thriving tiger population, surviving on the thousands of fallen soldiers just across the border.

Vietnam was often the testing ground for new types of weaponry and warfare. One unusual tactic tested was weather modification. Beginning in 1963, the U.S. began experimenting with cloud seeding, using silver iodide and various other chemicals. Although being able to control the natural environment has always been a goal of armies in battle, advanced technology brought what might seem like science-fiction scenarios closer to real life.

Weather modification was attempted to make roads and trails hard to travel, to disturb radar readings, and to cause floods and landslides. No information about the success of the weather-modification programs has ever been released by the Pentagon, and detailed information about the chemicals used is still not available. Long-term effects of weather-modification efforts are not known for certain, but experts cite such effects as flooding, landslides, and erosion, all leading, again, to sacrifice of animal habitat in addition to widespread damage to the land.

More practically, the military introduced two special-purpose weapons during the war—concussion bombs and fuel/air explosives, both of which became more widely used during the Persian Gulf War.

Concussion bombs were used in Vietnam for spot clearing, most often to provide a helicopter landing site even in the densest jungle. Experimental applications of the explosives began in 1967, with full-scale use by 1970. Concussion bombs are huge, weighing approximately 7.5 tons. They are filled with a thick mixture of ammonium nitrate and aluminum powder called a slurry. The bombs detonate about three feet above the ground, and while there is no resulting crater, the land is cleared, leaving a three- to four-acre landing area. Trees and other plant life are blown away and all exposed human life and wildlife within 1,300 feet of the explosion will be killed.

The second type of weapon introduced in Vietnam was fuel/air explosives—used only in experiments during the Vietnam War, but in actual combat in the Persian Gulf War. The explosives are designed to set off land mines and booby traps and have been used as antipersonnel weapons. These explosives burst on the ground, releasing a fuel. Detonation occurs after a delay that allows the fuel and air to mix. There is no crater, but a clearing of approximately 2.5 acres results. No plant or animal life survives in the immediate area, and there is only a 50 percent chance of survival in the surrounding twenty-five acres. In cases where the fuel/air explosive malfunctions, it explodes into a fireball, making wildfires possible.

CENTRAL AMERICA

American troops were involved in numerous military actions throughout the 1980s, in particular in Central America. The one big "hot spot" throughout the Reagan presidency was Nicaragua, a tiny tropical country in Central America. The U.S.-backed counterrevolutionaries, or Contras, fought a guerrilla war in the jungles of the small country. By 1986, the Contras began attacking the means of production, agricultural services, cooperatives, and state farms in Nicaragua's rural areas. The U.S. economic embargo against Nicaragua had already weakened the country; attacks against the rural people served a further blow. In an effort to support the people and feed the population, the Nicaraguan government established banana plantations in the mangrove forests. This effort to improve the economy, however, failed miserably when the loss of the wetlands (the mangrove forests) resulted in ruining the shrimp-farming industry and damaging numerous fisheries.

In another direct attack on the environment, resistance groups set fire to the forests and other profit-making environmental assets belonging to the Nicaraguan government. As in most guerrilla wars, resistance groups use any means available in their efforts to disrupt and defeat the government.

Government troops also used numerous tactics that proved detrimental to the environment. Aerial bombings damaged many forests and fields. A fragile lava bed became the site of a tank training ground.

Forest fires caused some of the most devastating damage of the war. Exploding munitions caused unplanned forest fires. Refugees attempting to live off the land often attempted slash-and-burn agriculture, which is characterized by massive burning of forested areas. Crops are planted for one season, then a new spot must be chosen, since the soil cannot sustain crops for extended periods. Often, even fertile farmland became overfarmed, and soil erosion became a severe problem. In 1983, retreating Contras started a forest fire in northern Nicaragua that burned uncontrolled for over a month, reducing to ashes an estimated 74,000 acres of pine forest.

Military presence in the region caused damage even when no actual fighting was taking place. Large areas of land were cleared for road building so the U.S. National Guard and other American military forces could transport equipment and also make room for military posts. Besides despoiling the land for military purposes, there have been rumors, according to The Environmental Project on Central America, that American soldiers shot wildlife for sport and frequently trapped live parrots to take with them back to the United States.

In a 1986 interview with *The Washington Post,* U.S. National Guard spokesman Joseph Hanley spoke of why the U.S. military preferred to conduct maneuvers in Honduras, along the Nicaraguan border. Hanley argued that the maneuvers offered the most realistic training available to National Guard troops, training they could not get in the United States. "If you're building a road, you don't have to worry about the width of the culverts, about the Environmental Protection Agency or about the environmentalists," Hanley told *The Washington Post.* Despite the efforts of top military leaders toward environmental reform, it seems that educating the field officers about the reasons behind environmental regulations remains a neglected area, even in the changing military.

Another indirect result of warfare, but one seldom

discussed, is the relaxation of environmental standards during war. This became a serious problem during the decade of fighting in Central America. Many measures to aid a threatened environment had taken place throughout Central America during the early to mid-1970s. With the onset of war in the late 1970s and throughout the 1980s, many conservation projects were halted or past efforts destroyed. For instance, in 1983 an estimated 154 square miles of a reforestation project were ravaged by Contra forces. Once-protected national forests were opened to firewood cutting, cattle grazing, and garbage dumping. The severe economic conditions and restrictions imposed by various boycotts made food a scarce resource. Poaching became a matter of survival for the impoverished people of the region.

Despite severe environmental problems that occurred during the decade of fighting, there was an unexpected increase in wildlife populations and a lessening of exploitation of some natural resources by outside corporations and governments.

While the battles raged on throughout the country, trade in gold, mahogany, cedar, animal skins, sea turtles, shrimp, and lobster nearly stopped. Forests were no place for hunters, who feared the guerrilla warfare that took place deep within the wilderness areas. Without human hunters, populations of white-tailed deer, peccaries, pacas, agoutis, monkeys, crocodiles, caimans, and iguanas increased dramatically. There was even a limited resurgence of populations of jaguars, ocelots, margays, manatees, and river otters.

Some areas of wilderness also saw relief during the

fighting. Although large portions of land were devastated by refugees searching for homes and land to cultivate, other areas were abandoned as potential cattle pastures by ranchers who took their large operations outside of Nicaragua.

PERSIAN GULF

One of the most recent accounts of direct environmental damage during war was a major episode of the 1991 Persian Gulf War. In an attempt to either stop an Allied invasion, shut down desalinization plants, or perhaps to destroy the Kuwaiti and Saudi economies, Saddam Hussein's Iraqi troops deliberately spilled millions of gallons of oil into the shallow gulf waters.

A couple of weeks later, as Allied troops moved in closer and Iraqi troops began to withdraw, Saddam Hussein apparently called for the systematic destruction of Kuwait's oil fields. Whether the aim was to destroy the enemy's economic base, was a last-ditch effort to stop the encroaching enemy, or was a strategic plan to stop Allied aerial bombings, Saddam's orders were planned well in advance. Detonators previously placed at strategic locations destroyed an estimated 1,250 oil wells and left close to 600 wells burning. The last fire was not extinguished until nearly nine months after the fires began.

Saddam Hussein's actual motives remain unclear. Without knowing his reasons, it could be assumed that Saddam's motives were similar to those of other leaders throughout history who have ordered attacks on the environment. Yet the question still arises: Was it an act of warfare, of using the environment to benefit his military objectives, or to deny resources to an enemy? On the other hand, could it have been terrorism? Did Saddam Hussein hold the environment hostage in the first case of environmental terrorism during war?

Since before American troops arrived in the Persian Gulf, as early as September 1990, Hussein had threatened to blow up oil wells if his presence in Kuwait was challenged. The attacks were carefully planned to do the maximum amount of environmental damage. In some instances, antipersonnel mines were placed around the wells to deter fire-fighting efforts.

The oil spills seem to have been no less deliberate, despite denials by Iraq. Burr Heneman of the International Council on Bird Preservation was in the Persian Gulf during 1991 working on clean-up efforts with the Saudi Wildlife Agency. According to Mr. Heneman, the spills attributed to the Iraqis seemed obviously intentional. In fact, Heneman pointed out that nozzles and valves were in place to aid in dumping the oil.

This seems to provide a significant insight into Hussein's motives. In earlier warfare, a leader did not tell the enemy of plans to flood fields, burn crops, or raze forests. There were no preparations to destroy something months in advance of the battle. The acts were part of warfare, sometimes intentional, sometimes accidental. It was assumed that the motives were revenge or the ultimate annihilation of the enemy or the idea that "If I can't have it, no one else will either."

Saddam Hussein raised the stakes of modern warfare. Like a terrorist holding his hostages at gunpoint until a payoff is delivered, Saddam voiced his threats to the world. He spoke openly of what he would do, of the harm he would cause if his conditions were not met. He made threats on the environment, held the Middle Eastern environment hostage, and followed through on his threats when the coalition forces did not meet his demands to leave him alone in Kuwait. When U.S. troops entered Kuwait, Saddam began efforts designed to destroy the environment. Some experts estimated the damage could wreak havoc on the entire world ecosystem.

If these acts were indeed acts of environmental terrorism, they were the first such deliberate acts against the earth. We cannot say for certain what Saddam's motives were, but a new precedent was nevertheless set, and the United States was quick to see the potential of this strategy. Frustrated by Saddam's refusal to withdraw immediately in the face of American involvement, the United States threatened to use the environment against Iraq. The people of Iraq depend for survival on the water that runs from the Tigris and Euphrates Rivers. The U.S. threatened to stop the water supply if Iraq did not back down. Although the threat was never carried out since victory came swiftly to the coalition forces, it was threatened as a consequence of aggression.

Whatever the motives, the Iraqi troops deliberately set out to destroy the desert and Persian Gulf ecosystems in a last desperate attempt during an unusual war. The long-term effects of the actions are not yet certain. In fact, many of the events of the war are still disputed. The actual amount of oil spilled in the gulf is not known. Conflicting stories on many of the aspects of the Persian Gulf War abound that will only be resolved over time. In addition to the spills caused by the Iraqis, the allies themselves were responsible for some of the oil pouring into the gulf, from the bombing of tankers.

The Persian Gulf ecosystem is fragile because of its unusually shallow water and the unusual conditions of the area. It includes sea grasses, salt marshes, mangrove swamps, mud flats, and some coral reefs. The Persian Gulf is dependent on the sea grasses that help stabilize the marine food chain. Fish, green turtles, and dugong feed on sea grass and shrimp, and pearl oysters feed on food found only in the sea grasses. A study conducted by the National Center for Atmospheric Research and the University of Washington studied the marine life in the gulf. Dr. Sylvia Earle, a biologist and the chief scientist for the National Oceanic and Atmospheric Administration, reported on the findings of that study in a *National Geographic* article. Dr. Earle found the sea grasses deep in the gulf still alive but coated with oil. The oil will eventually kill the sea grasses if the leaves and stems are smothered by it. Mollusks and crabs had not fared even that well, and these creatures were found dead and oil coated.

According to a booklet published by the United States government's Gulf Task Force, "many ecologically sensitive areas could not be protected." The report goes on to document damage to shore birds, some salt marshes, and shallow-water coral.

In addition to the grasses, effects of the spill are likely to be felt by a multitude of marine life. The gulf is home to shrimp (already threatened prior to the war), dugongs, dolphins, whales, green turtles, hawksbill turtles, sea snakes, crabs, and numerous other species. While some animals are more vulnerable than others, each depends on the gulf for food and habitat.

Another hard-hit species is the Socotra cormorant. It has been estimated that as much as 50 percent of the world's population of Socotra cormorants lived in the region prior to the war. According to Burr Heneman, some 20,000 birds, including all of the Socotra cormorants in the area—the northwest quadrant of the gulf region—were destroyed as a result of the oil spills and fires. Heneman points out that the main habitat area for shore birds was further south than the spill area, thereby saving untold numbers of birds.

The birds will be feeling the effects of the oil fires for some time to come, however. Thousands of migratory birds visit the Persian Gulf each spring. Immediately following the war, spring migration in 1991 was adversely affected by the smoke from burning wells. Birds found far south of Kuwait had oil on their plumage because, as scientists investigating the effects of the burning oil reported, even the smoke of the fires was oil-filled. Planes would emerge from the smoke streaked with oil. Concentrations of sulfur dioxide, nitrogen oxides, and various other pollutants were detected in the smoke by British researchers in March 1991. Another danger to the birds lies in the oil lakes still plentiful all over Kuwait. Throughout the desert, lakes of oil have appeared and beckon the unknowing birds, who never emerge from the oil.

The fires produce toxins in the atmosphere that revisit

the earth in the form of acid rain, which is deadly not only to marine and animal life but also to crops and native vegetation. High levels of acidity are expected to remain in the desert soil for a long time to come. As with other effects in the Persian Gulf, however, the long-term consequences have no way of being fully assessed at this time.

Besides the widely publicized damage from oil fires and the spills, there were numerous other environmental disasters during the Persian Gulf War. Animals were frequently the victims of the war. In most cases, the animals were killed in indirect attacks, merely by being in the way of the battle. Occasionally, animals were the direct target of the war and its players.

Prior to the war, Kuwait had a camel population of 10,000. That figure is now estimated at 2,000 camels. Desert warfare at night was often most treacherous for the camels. By night, the troops saw only blips on a radar screen. Assuming and fearing an approaching Iraqi enemy, the tank troops fired at and destroyed whatever caused the blips on the screen. It was not until the following morning, when the desert was strewn with dead camels, that the troops realized the blips had not been the enemy.

Replenishing the endangered Arabian oryx populations in Kuwait was an ongoing effort prior to the war. This program has come to a halt as a result of the war.

In a more direct assault on animal life, it was discovered by advancing Allied troops that Iraqi soldiers had destroyed the Kuwait City Zoo, killing and maiming the zoo animals. Out of a collection of over four hundred animals prior to the war, fewer than twenty-four could be found after the Iraqis left. The U.S. Army entering Kuwait City took on an unusual role for the military. A U.S. Army veterinarian, Colonel Philip Alm, began caring for the wounded and starving animals, finding food and water for them, and even removing bullets from some four-legged victims at the zoo.

The most disastrous consequences of the Persian Gulf War, however, may be less obvious. Heneman, studying bird populations for the International Council on Bird Preservation, stated the concern. "I believe the damage to the desert ecology has been far greater than the damage to bird and marine life." The thousands of military vehicles moving across the sand not only destroyed the fragile desert plants but broke through the desert's natural crust that helps lessen problems of wind and erosion. The digging of trenches and movements of troops added to the losses, as did bombing and strafing. The harm done by tanks in North Africa during World War II is still evident half a century later; the damage in Kuwait is not likely to disappear any more quickly. One immediate result will be in the increased severity of dust storms and the greater degree of erosion resulting from disturbing the sand. It has been estimated that as much as 25 percent of Kuwait's land surface has been devastated, and long-term effects may prove to be the most serious consequences of the Persian Gulf War.

The coalition forces bombed numerous chemical, biological, and nuclear facilities in Iraq throughout the Persian Gulf War. Although exact numbers have not been released by either side, and actual consequences of the attacks are not known, implications of such attacks are immense.

French troops reported detecting toxins on the Iraq-Saudi border, assumed to be from the bombed factories. The toxins were never identified, and reports indicated that the substances posed no danger to human health or the environment, but long-term effects of the release of any of these toxic substances into the atmosphere and the ground will not be known for perhaps decades.

Experts believe that bombings may have only partially ignited the chemicals in these plants, possibly leading to more severe problems later on. Cleanup of partially burned chemicals would be extremely dangerous. In addition, scientists believe that in some instances, the partial incineration may have created unstable and dangerous by-products, such as dioxin, which remain in the environment for a lengthy period of time.

Perhaps the gravest damage to the environment was the result of the longest war the U.S. ever waged—the Cold War. For nearly half a century, the United States fought a war of ideology, backed by some of the world's most technologically advanced, most powerful, most frightening, and most dangerous weapons. The Cold War had no single enemy, but it did involve combat—in Korea, Vietnam, and Central America. Yet even in "peacetime" there was conflict. Because of this unique situation, environmental damage resulting from the Cold War has been included in the section called "Environmental Dangers of Preparing for War." The Cold War and preparations for potential war became an easy excuse for allowing dumping of toxic wastes, chemical and biological weapons experiments, and nuclear weapons manufacturing and testing. There was unprecedented secrecy throughout the half-century of the Cold War; the effects reveal themselves gradually and are difficult to assess. Repelling Soviet and other nations' aggression and expansion seemed to justify whatever means were necessary. That destruction to the environment is a grim testimony to the military legacy of the last half of the twentieth century.

2.

ENVIRONMENTAL IMPACTS FOLLOWING WARFARE

WHILE ENVIRONMENTAL DESTRUCTION during warfare is often overlooked as the more immediate concerns of human death and loss of homes take center stage, after a war is over and countries are left to clean up the damage, ecological devastation often becomes more noticeable. In fact, following a war, there is often additional damage, much of it unaccounted for and never considered during the battle.

Numerous hazards cause environmental damage following a war. The abandonment of materials and explosives can be devastating. This might include battle areas strewn with supplies, debris, trash, perhaps even toxic chemicals. A major threat following warfare is the explosion of undetected munitions or the presence of radioactive residues on the battlefield. Further destruction can result from deforestation and erosion that worsens over time, long after fighting ceases. Often the gradual extinction of wildlife species is the last and most complete loss to an already devastated ecosystem.

ABANDONMENT OF MATERIALS AND ORDNANCE

Hollywood has made the image of a battlefield following war a familiar sight. Visions of cannon, guns, canteens, bombed-out tanks, fallen planes, and sunken ships are frequently images that the big screen has utilized to call up human sympathy for the plight of other humans following a war. Little thought was ever given to the environmental impacts of such symbolic items. Hollywood films never romanticized nor dwelled upon the hastily constructed buildings, the bunkers, the trash left after the fighting stopped and the victors returned home. Yet the "leftovers" of war are often among some of the most troublesome problems facing a recovering nation.

Let's look first at examples from American history. Bodies of the dead (both men and horses) were frequently left lying on the battlefields. This was especially a problem in the summer, when the heat made the situation more serious. Numerous United States National Park officials mention diaries and battle reports that described the hundreds of dead lying across fields. In several instances, both in the American Revolution and the Civil War, bodies were actually dumped in creeks to get rid of them. The military conscripts probably never knew that dumping the bodies into the creeks tainted the water supply for everyone downstream.

Battles also left debris scattered across the battlefields. Civil War–era equipment was heavy and cumbersome. If a retreating army had to leave an area quickly, or if too many troops were killed, much of the equipment had to be abandoned. One way to ensure that the enemy could never again utilize a cannon abandoned on the battlefield was to drive a spike through the cannon. The unusable piece of junk remained in place where it had last been fired.

Since the Revolution, sunken ships have been resting at the bottom of numerous rivers, seas, and oceans. The bottom of the York River, at the mouth of the Chesapeake Bay, is the grave of more than fifty warships sunk during the siege of Yorktown at the end of the Revolutionary War.

During the Civil War, ships were sunk off the Atlantic coast and all along the expanse of the Mississippi River. Perhaps the most famous ocean relic of the Civil War is the ironclad *Monitor* off the North Carolina coast.

During World War I, boats again littered the floor of the Atlantic Ocean, along with their cargo. More devastating than the ships, however, were the substances purposely dumped into the ocean following World War I. At the end of the war, the Germans were ordered to dump 20,000 tons of stockpiled chemical weapons into the Baltic Sea to dispose of them. Since that time, Danish fishermen have occasionally been poisoned with mustard gas leaking out of the rusty containers and into the sea.

Numerous ships sunk during World War II remain at the bottom of oceans. Sea battles took on a new importance during that war, and hundreds of oceangoing vessels were sunk during its course. Immediately following World War II, as the Cold War heated up and nuclear tests were conducted, other ships were sunk as part of those experiments. In addition to the ships sunk while in the water, there were hundreds of aircraft shot down during World War II over the oceans of the South Pacific.

Aside from the esthetic offense of ships half-submerged in waters and remaining as partially visible reminders of battle, there is a serious threat to marine life caused by the substances found on ships. Oil spills from sinking ships can often cause severe damage to ocean life and life along the shores. Other chemicals aboard ship, in addition to the products utilized daily by humans, are often pernicious to animal life. Normally, munitions found on ships that were sunk during wartime can present the same dangers as those dumped into the ocean.

A vivid example is found in the Skagerrak seabed between Norway, Sweden, and Denmark. It is known that at least twenty-one ships (some estimates run as high as fifty ships) loaded with German chemical weapons were sunk in the area. A commission formed at the end of the war decided that the quickest and cheapest way to dispose of the more than 300,000 tons of chemical weapons was to load them on damaged ships and sink them.

A 1984 report by the Danish Ministry of the Environment also claimed that between 36,000 and 50,000 tons of chemical ammunition had been dumped in the Baltic Sea by Soviet Occupation forces following World War II. It was also discovered that the Germans sank a ship containing 5,000 tons of nerve gas off the coast of Denmark just before the war ended. The Danish report further documented that a total of thirty-four ships and 151,425 tons of ammunition had been sunk in the Skagerrak in the three years immediately following the war.

Although scientists are uncertain what the long-term effects of the chemicals will be on the marine life, officials do know that the chemical containers are deteriorating undersea, and leaking containers have already been retrieved. Unfortunately, much of the mustard gas recovered is still potent and remains intact even in the disintegrating containers. The chemical reactions that occur as the mustard gas breaks down are often considered more toxic than the original mustard gas, and experts suggest these reactions may continue for as long as four hundred years. Denmark has been the most vocal of the three Scandinavian countries, and even began compensating local fishermen for damages in 1986. The Danish government is currently conducting studies to determine the long-term effects of the more than 300,000 tons of chemical weapons on the marine animal and plant life and the ocean ecosystem.

One of the most devastating and long-term consequences of modern war is unexploded ordnance. These munitions lying around areas where children often play make the news headlines frequently. While unexploded munitions pose a grave threat to humans, they are also a danger to the natural environment and to the wildlife that might be living among it.

Unexploded munitions are usually artillery and mortar shells, antitank and antipersonnel mines, bombs, and grenades. There are numerous reasons for unexploded munitions, such as hitting a soft surface (snow or mud), defective fuses, or improper assembly. Detecting these munitions after the war is over is a difficult problem. Munitions can last for many years undetected. In fact, there are shells and grenades remaining even today on the World War I site of the Battle of Verdun, which took place nearly eighty years ago.

World War II brought increased use of explosives. There were more mines laid in Poland during World War II, by both the Germans and the Allies, than in any other country. It has been calculated that 80 percent of the entire landmass of Poland was mined. As of 1985, according to a report presented to the United Nations Environmental Programme (UNEP) by Dr. Arthur Westing, 15 million mines had been discovered in Poland, and more continue to be discovered on a regular basis.

Another heavily mined area was Libya, where an estimated 5 million mines were placed. The areas of Libya most heavily mined were large tracts of arid land and rangeland. Since the end of the war, an estimated 125,000 domestic animals and an undetermined number of wild animals have been killed as a result of unexploded ordnance. Of that figure, 60 percent have been camels. In addition, many of the valuable water holes on the vast stretches of arid land were rendered inaccessible by the minefields.

Often the munitions are dumped near an old factory or are left abandoned. One example is an abandoned munitions plant in Hallschlag, Germany, about 100 miles west of Frankfurt on the Belgian border. A private company has been hired to clean up the site, at an estimated cost of $5.85 million. The project, which began in September 1991, is expected to take three years. There are estimates that 20,000 to 50,000 grenades litter the site, and 10 percent of them are believed to contain mustard gas.

The report to UNEP clearly outlines some of the dangers that these unexploded munitions present to the environment. In addition to the tragic loss of life that most often accompanies the unexpected explosions, there is a disturbance of the soil. Once the soil has been destroyed, there is long-term danger from erosion. Vegetation is destroyed, including trees and animal life. Wildlife habitat is threatened. According to the report to UNEP, gazelles in North Africa no longer live in areas that were mined during World War II.

Another danger from unexploded munitions lies at the bottom of various seas, ports, and rivers throughout the world. World War II sea mines have been found at the approaches to the Port of Le Havre, France, in the waterways of Berlin, in the Thames estuary in the United Kingdom, and even some sixty miles off the coast of North Carolina. The biggest danger to the environment, even greater than the danger from an actual underwater explosion and the related damage, is the explosive material in the munitions. For example, cyclonite, a common military explosive, is a nerve poison to mammals and is used commercially as a rat killer. Cyclonite remains active in sea water for many years without dissipating.

Since the end of World War II, 16 million artillery

shells, 490,000 bombs, and 600,000 underwater mines have been discovered in France. Despite the staggering number of discoveries, numerous areas are still closed in the 1990s, due to unexploded ordnance.

Modern technology and greater numbers of personnel and weapons have once again made problems of warfare more intense and longer lasting. Examples of remains of World War II lie on the Pacific Islands that were often the scene of bloody and fierce battles during the war. In 1975, William Bartsch made a trip throughout the Gilbert and Ellice Islands while doing research on the war remains in the Pacific. Even thirty years after the war, the remains were highly visible throughout the islands.

On the island of Funafuti, Bartsch found the "borrow pits" to be the most common reminders of the war. These large pits were dug to excavate coral for use in constructing runways and then became dumps for the withdrawing military at the end of the war. Today, these pits at each end of the island provide a grave for boiler tanks, vehicle chassis, tires, spare parts, and other junk the United States no longer had any use for.

Frequently on his trip through the chain of islands, Bartsch spotted wreckage of planes and LSTs (Landing Ship, Tank). On Nanumea, the northernmost Ellice atoll, an almost perfectly preserved LST is the first landmark visitors see. The LST had been loaded with supplies for the new base in the summer of 1943, but the small atoll was completely surrounded by a coral reef, which made landing directly on the beach impossible. In the desperate attempt to get the supplies to the troops, the LST was intentionally run aground on the coral reef, where it has remained to this day. Soon after the LST arrived on the atoll, the Americans blasted a narrow passageway through the coral to enable small boats and landing craft to maneuver their way to the beach to bring people and supplies. That passage remains the only clear opening to the beach today.

On Betio, also part of the Ellice Island chain, war remains are visible everywhere, rusting on the once-pristine beaches. Artifacts include an entire Sherman tank, bunkers, concrete blocks used to divert landing craft at the beaches' edge, and occasionally live munitions.

Poignant reminders of the war are also in the Aleutian Islands and lower Alaska Peninsula in the state of Alaska. According to the Corps of Engineers' *Draft Environmental Impact Statement for World War II Debris Removal and Cleanup,* compiled in 1979, the debris consists of a variety of materials. Such materials include "the remains of troop quarters, mess halls, gymnasiums, warehouses, power plants with engines and generators, ammunition magazines and bomb dumps, fuel depots, garages and workshops, airplane runways and hangars, hospitals, radio and weather stations, gun emplacements, bunkers, and miscellaneous material including live and detonated ordnance, vehicles and heavy machinery, pierced steel airstrip matting, barbed wire, communications and utility poles and cable, pipelines, antisubmarine nets, bedsprings, and 55-gallon POL [petroleum, oils, lubricants] drums." Due to the fact that defense and surveillance positions needed to be close to coastal areas during wartime, much of the debris is concentrated in the coastal areas.

War debris on the Aleutian Islands has contaminated

the islands' water supplies. The report emphasizes that there is constantly a supply of flowing fresh water. In fact, according to the report, "it is almost impossible to look in any direction without seeing a stream, river, pond, lake, or the sea." This has proved to be a substantial problem because of the large amount of rusting machinery, leaking POL drums, and other materials in and near the rivers, streams, lakes, ponds, and estuaries. One serious difficulty has been the rusting POL drums, which have released petroleum products into the groundwater. According to the report, items such as asphalt, grease, motor oil, paint, paper, fiberboard, plasterboard, rusting drums, sheet metal, tires, cable, insulating materials, and explosives and gunpowder have been found in the water on the Aleutian Islands. Enough coal was stockpiled on one island that the residents of the island continue to use the coal to heat their homes today—over forty-five years later.

The Environmental Impact Statement pointed out an interesting paradox facing the military. If the Aleutian debris is not removed, contamination and unsightly debris will remain in place indefinitely. If a cleanup program is initiated, the land will be disturbed in places where humans have not been since the end of World War II. Then there will be additional disruption of habitat and species, especially in the National Wildlife Refuges and the National Wilderness Preservation System established on the islands.

A similar dilemma concerns the sunken ships lying at the bottom of the world's oceans. Dr. Sylvia Earle of the National Oceanic and Atmospheric Administration studied Truk Lagoon in 1976. Dr. Earle discovered that the sunken ships still slowly leak oil and other contaminants into the surrounding waters. The slow leakage does not appear to be detrimental to marine life, and Dr. Earle believes it to be broken down sufficiently by the water. There are others who argue that even the slow leakage should be stopped, since there may be some unknown damage to plant and animal life. Dr. Earle's study points out, however, that if the ships are disturbed, the slow leak could become a major oil spill, which would be detrimental to the marine life that has become abundant on the sunken hull. Similarly, numerous unexploded mines will gradually erode, leaking small amounts of various acids and other toxic substances into the ocean waters over a long period of time. If those mines are detonated, however, damage to the surrounding plant and animal life would be catastrophic. The legacy of human warfare seems to linger on far into the future, challenging future generations to find answers for tragedies of the past.

Other dilemmas face the Vietnamese people today. Although the United States, with no diplomatic relations with Vietnam, does not participate in the cleanup efforts in Vietnam, the issues remain much the same. Numerous tanks, airplanes, and other remnants of the war are still evident today, all of which will remain unless physically removed. Sites where U.S. bases were located contain the remains of a modern civilization at war, such as petroleum products, solvents used to clean equipment, toxins used in the defoliation program, and numerous other poisons. Antitank and antipersonnel mines were used extensively during the Vietnam War and remain hidden deep in the jungles of Southeast Asia.

In the most recent war, in the Persian Gulf, reportedly thousands of tons of unexploded ordnance exist. The deserts of Kuwait and Iraq are somewhat unique, because the surface landing for the mines was often soft sand that blows and shifts continuously. This means that there were more unexploded bombs than in other circumstances, because of the soft landing spot. Blowing and drifting sands make it impossible to walk through a field and flag the unexploded bombs. The sands may cover the danger-ous object completely, only to uncover it again years from now. Another danger is that the object may still be close enough to the surface to detonate if it is walked on or driven over but not close enough to the top for detection. During World War II, metal detectors were utilized to help recover unexploded ordnance not readily visible on the surface. Detection is not always guaranteed today, how-ever, as more and more explosives are encased in plastic.

A recent government study estimates that 70 percent of the conventional bombs dropped over Iraq missed their target. Of the 88,500 tons of bombs dropped on Iraq, 17,700 tons, or 20 percent of the total, never exploded.

In addition to the traditional bombs scattered over the Kuwaiti and Iraqi deserts, an estimated 1 million unex-ploded Rockeye bomblets litter the U.S.-designated sector of the Kuwaiti desert—an area comprising only 1,207 square miles of the desert the United States is responsible for clearing. The difficulty with removing the Rockeyes is that they are small and not located in any particular pattern. As the bomblets are discovered, they are deto-nated on the site. It will be several years before the organ-ized cleanup is complete and many years after that—some experts estimate as many as forty—before the desert is considered safe.

One of the first areas to be cleared by the explosive experts was the Ahmed Al Jabar military airfield in Kuwait. Nine unexploded bombs were located at the site, ranging from 500 to 2,000 pounds, and a total of more than 70,000 tons of ammunition. Humans, animals, and plant life in the desert will long be paying the price for the triumph of U.S. military tactics in the region.

Another closely related problem is found in the deserts of Kuwait and Iraq. The A-10 Thunderbolt II close-air support aircraft and the M-1 Abrams tank both fire ammunition with depleted uranium projectiles. In the center of each bullet, or projectile, is a rod made of depleted uranium, called a penetrator. The depleted uranium provides greater impact than other types of projectiles. While the ammunition is intact, the uranium is completely surrounded with lead, thus containing the radioactive material. Upon firing, however, the lead is stripped away, leaving the uranium penetrator exposed. If the projectile hits a solid object, such as a tank, the penetrator disintegrates, leaving uranium dust. If the penetrator hits the ground, it stays basically intact.

While radiation from depleted uranium projectiles is low, there is an ongoing process to decontaminate Allied equipment that was hit by depleted uranium projectiles. Uranium-dust-covered tanks are returned to the United States for decontamination before disposal. There are no current plans to decontaminate Iraqi equipment exposed to depleted uranium.

Projectiles that missed their targets and landed in the

desert present another problem. While the exact amount of uranium in each projectile is classified information, each tank projectile includes approximately seven to eight pounds of uranium. In tests currently under way at Aberdeen Proving Ground, Maryland, and Yuma Proving Ground, Arizona, there is no discernible migration of the uranium from ammunition fired into the ground. At both test sites, there has been no detectable radiation poisoning of surrounding wildlife, soil, or vegetation. The study, only a small-scale representation of the actual combat conditions in the Middle East, will not be concluded until 1994. Until that time, questions remain largely unanswered, and the extent of the danger, if any, from the projectiles to both humans and the environment will remain at best—a guess.

Despite assurances from the U.S. government, the Kuwaiti government has asked to have all depleted uranium projectiles removed from Kuwaiti soil. Researchers at Aberdeen report that it is not uncommon for recovery of a single depleted uranium projectile to take up to one and a half hours, even though the specific impact area is known. Due to the enormity of such a project in a large battle zone still covered with unexploded munitions and plagued with blowing sands, the price would be astronomical, both economically and in the loss of life from the unexploded munitions. An agreement on this has not been reached, and one is not expected in the foreseeable future. In addition to the depleted uranium projectiles in Kuwait, Southern Iraq is plagued with the radioactive munitions as well. Chances are unlikely that efforts will be made by the U.S. or the other members of the Coalition governments to clean up the depleted uranium in Iraq.

The Persian Gulf War was somewhat different where waste disposal was concerned. For the first time in the history of warfare, the U.S. forces found themselves under the world's close scrutiny. It has been estimated that U.S. troops, eating two meals each day from the plastic MRE (Meals Ready to Eat) bags, would generate 6 million used plastic bags each week. The amount of trash generated by a force of close to half a million is astronomical. Today's technology has made everything disposable, and recycling efforts are not at the forefront of concerns during a war. Water comes in plastic bottles, soft-drink cans are aluminum, junk food is wrapped in cellophane and usually has an extra piece of cardboard to go along with it. A good portion of this trash will remain in the desert, the responsibility of Saudi Arabia and Kuwait to clean up. In addition to the garbage generated by the troops, there are the usual military wastes, such as solvents, acids, paint, fuel, lubricants, explosives. Each of these products could quickly pollute underground water, which the desert ecosystem depends on.

In each war, the solution has been to bury what could be buried, filling up huge, often hastily dug landfills. Many times the burial sites were left exposed, with huge holes of trash and debris marking the American exit from the site. What could not be buried was usually incinerated, often producing a stench that soldiers seem to remember forever. As greater numbers of troops are routinely gathered in one place and materials are designed to last forever without decomposing, problems of disposal after the war is over will grow more difficult.

Devastation on Tarawa after U.S. invasion, World War II. (Lowell
H. Beneke Collection. Courtesy of Admiral Nimitz State Historical Park,
Accession #92.510.009)

"Devil's Breath on Hell's Island," Iwo Jima, February 24, 1945.
(Defense Department photograph, U.S. Marine Corps. Courtesy of Admiral Nimitz State Historical Park, Accession #111828D)

Betio Island after navy bombardment, Tarawa, November 1943.
(OFFICIAL U.S. NAVY PHOTOGRAPH. COURTESY OF ADMIRAL NIMITZ STATE HIS-
TORICAL PARK, ACCESSION #111822.)

Guadalcanal, Japanese gas drums hit by shells. (FRITZ PAYNE COLLEC-
TION. COURTESY OF ADMIRAL NIMITZ STATE HISTORICAL PARK, ACCESSION
#90.542.010)

Saipan. A pockmarked battlefield on northern Saipan that the Fourth Marine Division wrested from the Japanese. Enemy trench at lower left. (U.S. MARINE CORPS PHOTOGRAPH. G. E. PETERS COLLECTION. COURTESY OF ADMIRAL NIMITZ STATE HISTORICAL PARK, ACCESSION #90.558.001dd)

Combres Hill, France, ca. 1918, World War I. (19 AIR SERVICE PHOTOGRAPHIC SECTION. U.S. ARMY AIR FORCE. NATIONAL ARCHIVES #018-E-3228)

Smashed by Japanese mortar and shellfire, trapped by Iwo's treacherous black-ash sands, amtracs and other vehicles of war lie knocked out on the black sands of the volcanic fortress,

February/March 1945. (U.S. COAST GUARD PHOTOGRAPH. NATIONAL ARCHIVES, #026-G-4474)

Gun crew from Regimental Headquarters Company, Twenty-third Infantry, firing 37mm gun during an advance against German entrenched positions, 1918. (U.S. ARMY PHOTOGRAPH. NATIONAL ARCHIVES #111-SC-94980)

Wreck of the U.S.S. *Maine*, 1898. (BUREAU OF SHIPS. NATIONAL ARCHIVES PHOTOGRAPH #019-N-19-9-17)

Hill 983, Bloody Ridge, September 6, 1951, Korean War. (U.S. ARMY PHOTOGRAPH. PHOTOGRAPHER PVT. JOHN C. PARKER. PHOTO #111-SC-379512)

Marines mopping up fire-swept Wolmi Island following the Inchon invasion, September 15, 1950. (DEFENSE DEPARTMENT PHOTO-GRAPH, U.S. MARINE CORPS. PHOTO #127-GK-234I-A2707)

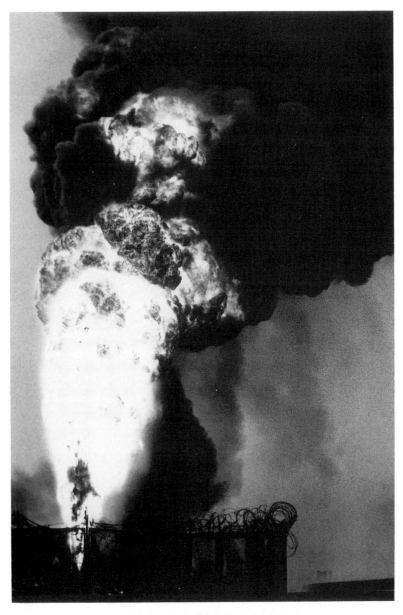

Kuwait. A burning oil well spews flame and smoke into the air after it was set afire by retreating Iraqi forces during Operation Desert Storm. (OFFICIAL U.S. NAVY PHOTOGRAPH, #DN-SN-91-07430)

DEFORESTATION AND EROSION

Deforestation and erosion are also serious problems facing countries following warfare. In addition to deforestation occurring during warfare, additional deforestation is usually required for rebuilding efforts and to support occupation forces. According to a 1946 report to General Douglas MacArthur, Supreme Commander for the Allied Powers, entitled "Natural Resources of Japan," approximately 500 million board feet of lumber and 100 million square feet of plywood were needed for occupation troops and family housing after World War II. Another 5 billion board feet of lumber would be required each year for five years to rebuild homes and businesses destroyed during the war.

Another serious side effect of deforestation is the possible extinction of animal species. The major cause of animal deaths after warfare is destruction of the habitat. Even those animals surviving a war may find it difficult to survive for any extended period of time with the native habitat destroyed and hopes for any resurgence of the habitat gone.

There was massive deforestation in Europe during and immediately following World War II. Great effort has been made to reforest these areas, although complete recovery of forest ecosystems may take several centuries.

It has proven easier in the past to rehabilitate agricultural lands and grasslands than tropical areas and forests. Following damage to grasslands and agricultural lands during World War II, recovery projects have focused on planting cover crops, reestablishing drainage patterns, and planting fruit trees and other crops. All of these activities bring erosion under control.

In tropical areas, recovery has been more difficult and is an ongoing process. The tropical soil does not hold nutrients as well, and long-term damage is more common. Overall recovery may take more than one hundred years.

Land-clearing techniques used in Vietnam—from bombing to Rome plows, Agent Orange to napalm—had more long-term consequences than any single war in American history. Those consequences are still obvious today in Vietnam. Vietnamese experts estimate that nearly 5.5 million acres of forest and one-fifth of the agricultural land were destroyed by bombings, land clearing, defoliating, and napalming during the war. Reclaiming that land, plagued by serious erosion and the takeover of "American grass" in once forested areas, is a slow process. Vietnam's hilly terrain seems to have been especially susceptible to erosion, and the trees have not grown back in the cleared areas, where the land is often as hard as concrete.

Deforestation is not always a direct result of defoliation or land clearing during war. In the aftermath of a decade of guerrilla fighting in Nicaragua and Honduras, deforestation has been caused indirectly by warfare. For more than a decade now, the Nicaraguans have watched their economy collapse in the midst of fierce battles. Today, thousands of Nicaraguans are searching for farmland. Their search leads them to the backcountry, where they cut down trees in areas once preserved as wilderness. It is estimated that more than 200,000 people were relocated to the hardwood forests of the north and the rain forests of the south. Deforested areas are facing serious erosion problems, and dust storms are becoming more common.

People attempting to live in the devastated areas, who once relied on agriculture and crops for survival, pose a threat to wildlife. For example, The Tropical Conservation Newsbureau reports that there is no shortage of guns in Nicaragua following the decade of fighting and that poaching of wild animals goes on unchecked.

The U.S. invasion of Panama in 1990 has had similar effects on that tiny Latin American country. Prior to the U.S. invasion, Panama boasted one of the most extensive national park systems in Central America. The country's fifteen national parks, which covered 11 percent of its land, constituted the only preserved land in the country. With the invasion of Panama, restrictions in the national park lands were eased, and even those areas are now threatened. Deforestation and poaching in the protected areas have become serious postinvasion problems.

A significant threat was posed to Panama's unprotected land by the U.S. invasion and the economic embargo prior to the actual invasion. The blockade was devastating to the Panamanian economy, forcing the starving peasants out of the cities and into the rain forests. Following the invasion, as thousands of Panamanians feared for their lives and faced homelessness, the forests again became a refuge. It is estimated that 3,325 acres of rain forest are destroyed each week in Panama as a direct result of subsistence farmers and reckless ranchers.

OIL FIRES IN THE PERSIAN GULF

The Persian Gulf War poses a number of new and difficult problems. Environmental hazards following the Persian

Gulf War are primarily the results of oil fires and oil spills throughout the gulf region that occurred during the actual fighting. Smoke from the burning oil contained polycyclic aromatic hydrocarbons and trace metals such as nickel, chromium, and vanadium, all of which are known or suspected to cause cancer in animals and humans. Whether the fires were serious enough to cause long-term damage to the animal population will not be known for many years.

Although the smoke from the fires was not as extensive as early predictions suggested, it will have a long-term negative effect on the region. The smoke contains sulfur dioxide and nitrogen oxides that collect in the atmosphere and return to the surface as acid rain. The area's sandy soils are not acid tolerant, making agricultural conditions worse than in more tolerant areas. Water supplies are also in danger of contamination from the acid rain.

POSITIVE EFFECTS FOLLOWING WARFARE

Despite the tragedies of warfare, there are ironically some positive effects of warfare as well, although these positive effects are usually far outweighed by the negative impacts. One of the often-overlooked effects of the Civil War is the impact on our National Park System. Forming a portion of the national parks in the United States today, many of the Civil War battlefields have been set aside for the enjoyment of millions of visitors each year. The land has been preserved and development had been somewhat slowed. Standing on the hill overlooking the field where Pickett's charge took place just outside of Gettysburg, Pennsylvania, can be a humbling experience for American visitors who take the time to stop and reflect on the battle that was fought there and all it represented.

Scavengers always seem to do well during wartime, when there is ample food for them. One intriguing story is of the vultures in Gettysburg. Today, hundreds of vultures winter in Gettysburg, Pennsylvania. Their nests are in the trees overlooking some of the bloodiest battle sites of Gettysburg. Between July 1 and July 3, 1863, more than 51,000 Union and Confederate troops were killed or wounded on the Gettysburg Battlefield. Never before that deadly battle, according to local legend, did the vultures winter in Gettysburg. On a January day in 1992, vultures did indeed circle over the battlefield known as the Devil's Den. A slow rain drizzled over the tangled masses of trees and vines, the winter landscape adding to the bleak battle-field mood. According to a National Audubon Society study in the early 1980s, approximately 900 birds now winter in Gettysburg each year. One explanation for the phenomenon is tradition. The original vultures found ample food on the Gettysburg Battlefield in the winter of 1863, and the birds' descendants have been returning to the area ever since.

Sea battles endured by American forces have left re-mains of those oceangoing vessels scattered throughout the world's seas. The serious adverse effects of the sunken ships are not to be overlooked, yet there are often unex-pected positive effects. Ships and aircraft of yesterday's battles have, in some cases, become undersea habitats for colonies of marine plant and animal life. In a 1988 *National Geographic* article, author Peter Benchley wrote of his surprise at the marine world surviving amid the wreckage of war. He wrote of the sea bringing forth new life out of the tragedies of the past, and how planes and ships have become reefs, housing many species of marine life. Even amid the rifles, gas masks, helmets, and boots of nearly half a century ago, life remains a vital force, and nature seems somehow stronger than humans could ever comprehend.

The results of Dr. Earle's research of the Truk Islands appeared in the May 1976 issue of *National Geographic*. Dr. Earle realized that Truk offered something not usually found—a unique opportunity to study an artificial reef in action. The exact age and condition of each of the sunken vessels was known and documented prior to Dr. Earle's study, making her findings even more valuable. Researchers found the sunken ships home to numerous species of coral, which in turn housed communities of fish, crabs, polychaete worms, and algae. In her dives to eleven of the wrecks, Dr. Earle counted more than a hundred species of algae, which included fifteen previously unknown species. Once again, the resiliency of nature seems to present itself where it is least expected. Many scenes of carnage have been declared historical monuments, such as Truk Lagoon in the middle of the Pacific Ocean. There is still, however, much controversy over the sunken vessels, with arguments raging about the safety of the underwater coffins.

The seas received some benefits from the war even during the midst of the fighting. During the war, commercial fishing operations came to a halt. In the years immediately following the war, there were many more fish, and the fish were generally much larger than those prior to the war. Populations of haddock, plaice, ling, and hake were increased during the war, and the Newfoundland harp seal populations increased rapidly, although the populations were diminished rapidly at the end of World War II.

Certain species of land animals thrived during World War II, in another unexpected and perhaps positive effect of the war. For example, gray wolf populations in Russia and Europe grew significantly during World War II. During the German occupation of Norway, local citizens were not allowed any firearms and therefore were not allowed to hunt. There was a surge in the populations of bears, foxes, and wolverines as a result.

One of the most beneficial areas to animals has been the Korean demilitarized zone (DMZ). A two-mile-wide strip of mountainside, stretching for some 151 miles across Korea, became a buffer between North and South following the Korean War. This area, containing marshes, meadows, oak, pine and maple forests, is a habitat to lynx and numerous previously endangered animals. The area today is home to nearly the entire world population of red-crowned cranes—plus mallards, geese, golden eagles, and white-tailed sea eagles.

RECLAMATION AND RESTORATION

There are often massive reclamation efforts at the end of a war, greatly improving the conditions of the area. It seems that humans are aghast at the destruction done once the fighting has stopped and they try to undo some of the damage. As was mentioned in an earlier section, often the task of restoration must be weighed against the consequences of leaving the damage. Restoration and cleanup of the war materials on the Aleutian Islands is one such example. Of course, the need to clean up this harsh wilderness was not recognized until twenty years after the fighting stopped. If the cleanup efforts had been part of the withdrawal, much of the dilemma facing government experts today would have been avoided.

Restoration projects were also initiated in the South Pacific and Japan, although the reasons behind them were often political, economic, and military rather than specifically for the environmental. In October 1945 the Natural Resources Section was established as a special staff section of General Headquarters, Supreme Commander for the Allied Powers, under the direction of General Douglas MacArthur. The Natural Resources Section was to inform MacArthur of any policies in Japan involving agriculture, fisheries, forestry, and mining.

Massive agricultural reforms were initiated in Japan, a country where too many people lived on too little land. The reforms were not begun out of sympathy or concern but rather out of fear. In a 1948 article for *Science*, Lieutenant Colonel Hubert Schenck, chief of the Natural Resources Section under General MacArthur, outlined the reasons behind the land reforms. It was believed that the Japanese had shown aggressive tendencies and initiated the attacks of World War II specifically because they sought out more land for expansion. If the Americans could show the Japanese how to manage their natural resources better, it was believed that future war would be averted and the Japanese would be content to stay in their own country with no further aspirations for more land.

Perhaps the most impressive strides toward recovery and reclamation are taking place today in Vietnam. There are major efforts under way to fill the thousands of huge bomb craters throughout the Vietnamese countryside and to discover unexploded ordnance. According to Elizabeth Kemf, who traveled in Vietnam between 1985 and 1988 and studied the environmental impacts of the war, Vietnam's Ministry of Forestry has developed a ten-year plan that will eventually reforest 3.7 million acres of barren hillsides. A national conservation plan calls for the planting of 500 million trees annually. Schoolchildren are contributing to the plan by planting an estimated 50 million trees each year.

Following the war, the Vietnamese realized that a vital part of the environment, the Plain of Reeds, was not recovering. The land could not support plant life. Without plant life, birds and other wildlife could not return. The only hope for recovery lay in keeping the moisture in the former wetlands, so dikes were rebuilt to hold in some of the moisture from the monsoon season.

Cajeput trees are also being gradually restored in the Mekong Delta. To date, thousands of acres of land have been planted with the mighty trees, which are somehow able to withstand and counter the high acid levels left in the delta. Gradually, wildlife has begun to return. Fish again swim in the waters of the delta, and floating rice is once again at home there. The best news came in 1986, when the Eastern

Sarus crane reappeared in the area. The crane is held sacred in Vietnamese culture, so its reappearance was a special victory. A crane preserve has been established and currently covers more than 22,000 acres in Vietnam.

Amidst the tragedies of the Cold War, several actions have been taken to reclaim and restore the prior condition of the land in areas throughout the United States used for testing or nuclear weapons production. In southern Indiana, numerous species of wildlife have found a haven of sorts on the army's 55,000 acres of land called Jefferson Proving Ground, or JPG. JPG tests about 85 percent of the army's conventional munitions. The land is littered with unexploded ordnance, making it necessarily off-limits to humans. In the absence of humans, the animals have thrived, despite an occasional mishap with an animal and exploding munitions. Officials at JPG report a dramatic increase in the numbers of animals roaming the army grounds. There are now populations of endangered reptiles as well as bobcats, deer, coyotes, and foxes.

Rocky Mountain Arsenal outside Denver has become a similar wildlife preserve despite the odds. There are now bald eagles, deer, coyotes, and herons wandering the high plains only a short distance from the urban sprawl of downtown Denver. Colorado Congresswoman Patricia Schroeder has been a long-time advocate of converting the Rocky Mountain Arsenal into an urban wildlife refuge to preserve the 17,000-acre site for the animals that live on the land despite the military's legacy. The government recently approved transfer of the site to the Department of the Interior following cleanup, making it the nation's largest urban wildlife refuge.

Aberdeen Proving Ground in Maryland has been busy setting up areas of the army's land as a wildlife refuge. The biggest success on the facility has been the eagle population. Closely monitored by Jim Pottie, a biologist at Aberdeen, the bald eagle population has been steadily increasing over the past several years. The 1991 annual survey located thirty-eight adult and twenty-seven young bald eagles, along with a golden eagle, on the grounds at Aberdeen. The Environmental Management office at Aberdeen reports that the eagles seem to have adapted quite well to the noise of maneuvers and the weapons tests at the base. Of course, Aberdeen provides the only nonurban area for miles along the eastern coast, giving the eagles little choice in their dwindling natural surroundings.

3.

ENVIRONMENTAL DANGERS OF PREPARING FOR WAR

WHILE THE ACTIVITIES of the military during and after a war are detrimental to the environment, activities of the military as it prepares for future warfare can cause severe environmental damage as well.

One of the first effects of military buildup is a relaxation of environmental standards. Prior to World War I, the United States had begun enacting legislation aimed at protecting the environment and conserving natural resources. Under the administration of Theodore Roosevelt between 1901 and 1909, 140 million acres was added to the National Park System. Legislation protecting land and water was passed. Big-game and bird preserves were established. As we prepared for war, much of the legislation was overturned or ignored when claims of patriotism overrode environmental controls. National parks were opened to grazing, logging, hunting, and agricultural development that had been restricted in the early 1900s.

The pattern was repeated during the rapid military buildup prior to the U.S. entry into World War II. In an essay for *Science* magazine in 1943, Henry B. Ward pointed to the serious situation created when the U.S. relaxed environmental standards in the name of national security. Ward cited contamination and waste and warned that the country would someday "pay for today's bad habits and thoughtless waste."

Lumber restrictions also were relaxed during World War II. Throughout American history, whenever wartime production increased, there has been little monitoring of pollution levels or controlling timber cutting.

The role of preparing for war changed dramatically in the post–World War II years. The onset of the Cold War brought daily military rehearsals for the Big War that everyone hoped would never come but decided to prepare for anyway. The military became a fixed part of American life, indeed an entire industry was built up around military preparations for war. By the end of the Cold War, there were a total of 1,246 military bases both in the United States and on foreign soil, seventeen nuclear warhead production sites operated by the Department of Energy, and twelve chemical weapons production and storage facilities. In addition to these official facilities are the hundreds of private corporations, research facilities, and universities involved in military-related matters.

TOXIC CONTAMINATION

A serious environmental threat as the military prepares for war comes from toxic contamination. In the daily operations of military bases, little thought was given to the storage and disposal of toxic substances until the past few years. While the military has begun taking precautions to contain and reduce toxic substances, the damage has already accumulated over more than forty years. Denver's Rocky Mountain Arsenal is considered one of the most toxic sites on earth and has been dubbed by the media "the most toxic square mile on earth." All of the toxic by-products from the production of mustard gas, napalm, incendiary weapons, and other types of munitions were dumped on the land for decades. Toxic ponds are lethal to wildlife, and poisons leaked into the groundwater for years before officials admitted there was even a problem at the arsenal.

According to a Defense Department report to Congress in February 1991, Rocky Mountain Arsenal is contaminated with pesticides; mustard gas and nerve agents; mercury; lead; arsenic; organic and inorganic chlorides; hydroxides and fluorides; solvents; acids; and a host of other toxic substances. Already, 8.5 million gallons of liquid and 500,000 cubic yards of soil have been removed from the arsenal. It has been estimated that cleanup may take as long as thirty years, and the remedy will cost U.S. taxpayers $2 billion. The tragedy is that the toxic wastes, even when they are removed from the arsenal, must go somewhere. The substances are so toxic that the United

States has no safe and permanent way to dispose of them at this time.

In addition to the chemicals poisoning the arsenal, there are unexploded bombs lying on and buried just under the surface of a former testing range. In the distance, the multi-million-dollar, five-story production plant stands like a cement memorial on the Colorado plains, where it will remain abandoned—a silent monument to the legacy of the Cold War.

Rocky Mountain Arsenal does not stand alone as an isolated case. Estimates are that more than 20,000 sites of present and former government lands are contaminated with toxic substances. Although the Department of Defense has begun the Installation Restoration Program, which was initiated in 1984, there are still discrepancies between what the U.S. government says it will cost to clean up the mess and what public advocates say it will cost. According to the Defense Department in a report entitled *Estimate of Cost to Complete the Installation Restoration Program*, released in October 1988 by the MITRE Corporation, it will cost approximately $4.8 billion to clean up the bases. According to the Center for Defense Information, a nonprofit organization that supports an effective defense while opposing excess expenditures, the cleanup bill could reach or exceed $150 billion. No matter what the actual cost of the cleanup, the detriment to the environment will most likely never be fully assessed or reversed.

Cherry Point Marine Corps Air Station at Cherry Point, North Carolina, is an example of an area where cleanup will be close to impossible. Throughout the Cold

War, industrial wastes were routinely dumped into the local creeks. Today, the creeks in the area contain high levels of toxic substances—such as mercury and lead. Fish here show signs of contamination and reproductive problems.

Another example of the toxic troubles caused by the expanding military is Aberdeen Proving Ground, Maryland. At the site that used to be known as Edgewood Arsenal, military and civilian personnel dumped a number of toxics, such as arsenic, cyanide, and napalm at the arsenal. The situation came to a head in May 1989 when three civilian managers for the U.S. Army Chemical Research, Development, and Engineering Center at Aberdeen were convicted for their part in the illegal disposal of the toxics.

The three high-ranking employees were convicted of knowingly allowing various chemicals to be improperly stored at the facility. According to court records, the three workers ignored repeated warnings by inspectors to remove the chemicals from leaky barrels they were stored in. There were even documented cases of deliberate dumping of hazardous materials into drainage pools. According to the Department of Defense's own account, officials have detected white phosphorous, arsenic, napalm, and other chemical agents. One of the major dangers at Aberdeen is its close proximity to state-designated critical habitat areas, a national wildlife refuge, and Chesapeake Bay.

Other less-publicized areas offer similar horror stories. Tinker Air Force Base just outside Oklahoma City was built in a major drainage basin and over central Oklahoma's only underground aquifer. Tinker Air Force Base has long been the repair depot for aircraft, weapons, and engines. The base is contaminated with solvents such as trichloroethylene and heavy metals like haxavalent chromium. According to the February 1991 report to Congress on the Defense Department's Installation Restoration Program (IRP), the contamination now covers 220 acres of base land and there are six landfills containing 1,705,000 cubic yards of industrial and sanitary waste. In addition to that, contamination has been identified at two industrial pits, one pond, two fire training areas, five radioactive waste disposal sites, twelve fuel sites, and three on-base creeks.

The Report on the IRP reads something like a recipe for the world's most toxic substances, and there is no discrimination against any geographic area:

· Anniston Army Depot, Alabama—Volatile organic compounds, heavy metals, paints, acids, solvents, degreasers, oil, and grease contaminate surface and groundwater.

· Hill Air Force Base, Utah—More than fourteen volatile organic chemicals such as benzene, methyl ethyl ketone, and ethanes, along with other hazardous and municipal wastes have contaminated groundwater. Contamination has been discovered off base as well, in a shallow underground aquifer, a water retention pond, and a natural spring.

· Treasure Island Naval Station, Hunters Point Annex, San Francisco, California—This navy shipyard, originally built in 1869, has tested positive for a number of toxins in the groundwater. Tests in 1987 detected benzene, PCBs, toluene, and phenols in the water. Studies also discovered higher than normal levels of heavy metals and other substances in offshore sediments. Despite these findings, a bottling company draws water from a spring located one mile from the annex, and the waters around the base are used for recreational activities, commercial navigation, and fishing.

- Twin Cities Air Force Reserve Base (Small Arms Range Landfill), Minneapolis, Minnesota—There have been ten sites identified at the Twin Cities Air Force Reserve Base as contaminated. The largest area is the actual landfill, which served the base from 1963 until 1972. The landfill, occupying three acres adjacent to the Minnesota River, contains the base's general refuse in addition to paint thinners and removers, paint, primers, and leaded fuel sludge, and is located within the 100-year flood plain and 500 feet from the Minnesota Valley National Wildlife Refuge. In Minneapolis-St. Paul 64,700 people depend on underground water located within a three-mile radius of the landfill for their drinking water.

In addition to the landfill, nine other sites of contamination have been identified, including fuel spills, sludge burial pits, hazardous waste drum storage areas, battery shop leaching pit, and an underground storage tank. Contaminants already identified include methylene chloride, dichloroethylene, acetone, butane, chloroform, trichloroethylene, benzene, and toluene.

Toxic contamination is not limited to the continental United States. American military bases worldwide are further sites of contamination. By the end of 1990, the army had identified 358 contaminated sites at European bases. The air force was anticipating ten to twenty sites on each European base as well. As in the United States, contamination is the result of fuel leaks, solvents, hazardous substances in landfills, and the ammunition at various firing ranges.

The United States is not the world's only toxic polluter. The former Soviet Union had a military-industrial complex that rivaled that of the United States. Levels of pollution generated in the USSR far surpassed that of the pollution created by the United States. One of the major causes of toxic poisoning in today's Commonwealth of Independent States is pollution. Without even the limited controls found in the United States, the Soviets could freely pour contaminants into the atmosphere for the past five decades. The Lenin Steelworks alone spewed out enough pollution to cover 4,000 square miles.

The countries of Europe are beginning to protest. Norway claims that a nickel-smelting factory near the Norwegian border creates more pollution in Scandinavia than all of the industries in Norway. The Soviet military-industrial complex stretches far into other areas of Europe as well. Perhaps the hardest hit are those countries that were once satellites of the former power.

The air in what was once East Germany is heavy with sulfur and dust, and it is believed that more than 10 million tons of toxic wastes are in local landfills. Cheap fertilizers heavy in phosphates have poisoned the land and water in

Czechoslovakia, leaving behind high, toxic levels of cadmium. Throughout eastern Europe, wastes are dumped into the same rivers and aquifers that supply drinking water to the people.

Cleaning up the mess in eastern Europe will be difficult if not impossible. In countries struggling to keep even a majority of their citizens fed, there is no money for cleanup of environmental disasters—indeed there is no money to even bring current practices up to safe levels. For example, Poland has estimated that it will take $400 million to halt ongoing environmental damage and another $25 billion to reverse the damage. The country cannot even pay the $400 million. The newly unified Germany must find a way to raise the $40 billion to $150 billion the government believes will be necessary to clean up the land, air, and water pollution there; and that does not cover the cost of toxic cleanup of the landfills.

It will be a long time, if ever, before the toxic poisons are cleaned up. Estimates are that it will take at least thirty years and $400 billion in today's dollars to clean up the mess caused by the U.S. military, and cleanup in the former Soviet Union will cost hundreds of billions more.

MUNITIONS TESTING

Another problem that holds serious implications both for human safety and the safety of the land, air, water, and wildlife is the unexploded ordnance found at numerous military installations. One of the biggest problems is that unexploded munitions are not considered toxic substances. This means that cleanup of the munitions is not covered under the Resource Conservation and Recovery Act that is paying for the cleanup of other contaminated sites.

Perhaps the worst case of unexploded ordnance is at the Army's Jefferson Proving Ground in Indiana. Jefferson Proving Ground has been a munitions test area since 1941. In the ensuing fifty years, the military test-fired an estimated 23 million rounds of ammunition. Today, officials estimate that 1.5 million of those test rounds remain unexploded, littering the facility's 55,000 acres. There are reportedly munitions buried 24 feet beneath the earth's surface. It must also be kept in mind that the military tests weapons on an ongoing basis. While the cleanup of toxic materials has been supplemented by a more careful policy of storing and disposing of those substances, that is not the case with munitions testing. The problem continues daily even as the military seeks a way to clean up the messes of the past.

MANEUVER DAMAGE

Preparations for warfare involve increased levels of mock-war exercises. Prior to World War II, the United States had never engaged in preparations for war at the level it did for World War II and the Cold War. While the level of military preparedness fluctuated with public opinion prior to World War II, the available technology did not allow the concentration of power found in World War II and ensuing years, even in times of high public support for a large military.

One of the major differences before and after World War II was in the amount of space required for an army (or navy or air force) to train. Even in World War II, only 4,000 acres were necessary for full-scale tank and infantry maneuvers. Today, army officials claim to need 80,000 acres to carry out similar exercises.

During World War II, troops under General George S. Patton held tank maneuvers in the southern California desert. Today, those tracks still remain visible. In most areas, only about 35 percent of the vegetation has recovered. In some places that were heavily utilized, only about 18 percent of the vegetation has recovered today.

Tank damage continues to be a major cause of environmental damage. Tanks destroy vegetation, wildlife habitat, and wildlife. Annual exercises are held in Germany that cause severe damage. Each year, hundreds of thousands of dollars in damage are done to the German countryside from the estimated 5,000 ground maneuvers carried out annually, including the annual "Reforger" exercise.

Reforger brings together large numbers of U.S. troops, many shipped in from National Guard bases in the States, to conduct field training in the German countryside. Thousands of U.S. Army and National Guard troops exercise for approximately two weeks, in cooperation with the other services, tearing up fields and roads. In the damp German countryside, it is not unusual for the combination of rains and tanks to turn fields into giant mud traps. In recent years, exercises have often come to a standstill when conditions grew too bad to maneuver even the tanks through. The maneuvers are not restricted to military bases but extend into the fields and planted crops of the German farmers and into the German forests.

Bases throughout the United States are subject to tank damage as well. Quantico Marine Corps Base in Virginia is heavily marked with tank trails, and often erosion is the result of breaking up the topsoil with military vehicles. At Fort Bragg Army Post in North Carolina, maneuver damage and fire-fighting measures have threatened the habitat—and the actual survival—of the already endangered red-cockaded woodpecker.

The military has recently proposed using the air space over four separate western areas for maneuvers. Much of the proposed land is wilderness or is currently under study as proposed wilderness areas. This is creating a new rift between residents of the western United States and the military.

Governor Cecil Andrus of Idaho proposed acquiring 150,000 acres of land in the Owyhee Canyonlands to be transferred to the Idaho National Guard. Under the terms of the negotiations, the U.S. Air Force would then be allowed to use the area as a practice bombing site. While no live bombs would be dropped, supersonic flights would be made at 10,000 feet, subsonic flights would occur at altitudes of only 100 feet, and chaff and flares would be dropped. Chaff is aluminum-coated fibers, about the same thickness as hair, used to deflect radar. It is dangerous to livestock, fish, and wildlife if eaten. The effects of the sonic flights on wildlife are not known.

In Utah, the military has proposed a similar plan. The air force wants a 200-mile corridor across Utah's canyonlands for training purposes, passing within three miles of Capitol Reef National Park. Each day, two B-52 and two B-1B bombers would pass over the area at approximately 500 feet above the ground.

The Colorado Air National Guard wants to establish a military operations area (MOA) in the Great Sand Dunes National Monument. The national guard estimates that fifty fighters, two to six bombers, and ten support aircraft would use the MOA twenty-four times each year, flying at heights of about 100 feet. Chaff and flares would also be used in the simulated attacks. The forest service argues against the proposal, fearing that the chaff and flares would impair water quality and would be dangerous to wildlife. The forest service also argues that the low flights would adversely affect migrating herds of bighorn sheep and elk in the area, along with obstructing the migration paths of waterfowl.

Perhaps the largest land proposal is in Alaska. The military wants to conduct maneuvers both on land and in the air at numerous national parks, preserves, and monuments. According to the National Parks Conservation Association, the military has proposed low-level flights; ground maneuvers across wetland areas, rivers, and tundra; and the use of live ammunition for the Alaska training area.

Plans are going forward in all four areas despite public outcry.

In other cases the military seems to be making the effort to consider the public's environmental concerns. The Department of Defense employs about one hundred civilian foresters and two hundred other natural resource experts, such as biologists and soil conservationists. Efforts are being made to lessen the environmental damage on military installations, and recent changes have been made to the rules governing maneuver damage.

For example, according to Army Lieutenant Colonel Gary Thomas of Deputy Assistant Secretary Baca's office, all tank troops have to undergo intensive environmental training. "Before a unit goes to the field and trains, they are required to get an environmental briefing," Thomas stated in a 1992 interview. He went on to discuss what the army is doing to reinforce the idea of stewardship. "They go over it—we've got this plot of land that's been entrusted to the department to use; we must take proper care of it. Here are the things this unit needs to do to make sure the land gets appropriate use. The services have produced videos both here in the States and overseas on what you can and cannot use, the maneuvering you can and can't do. Where the sensitive areas are, where endangered species are, and so on."

Lieutenant Colonel Thomas was hopeful that the environmental awareness in training will carry over into actual combat situations.

At the Piñon Canyon Training Area in Southern Colorado, the land has been divided into five parcels. Training is then cycled through the different parcels, avoiding ongoing training in the same spot.

It seems obvious from speaking with military officials that much of the change is a result of public opinion and federal laws. The major environmental concerns of the military continue to be the environment's impact on the troops. Colonel Cornelius commented that it is "in a commander's best interest" to be aware of such issues as sanitation procedures in the field and to learn to "live with your environment, not against it."

Even now, however, there is still ample evidence of the "human versus nature" concept of warfare. An article in a January 1991 issue of *The Journal of the American Medical Association* spoke of troops in the Persian Gulf battling the environment. The article compared environmental forces such as temperature, insects, sunlight reflected on the sand, and diseases to the threat of death from actual combat. In a November 1991 letter to the author concerning this book, Lieutenant Colonel Conrad H. Busch, responding on behalf of General Colin Powell, Chairman of the Joint Chiefs of Staff, commented, "General Powell is most concerned about the environment and its impact on defense issues."

CHEMICAL AND BIOLOGICAL WEAPONS PROGRAM

Chemical weapons are fast-acting poisons used to kill or injure enemy troops. The weapons range in potency from relatively mild harassing agents—such as tear gas—to blood agents and blister agents—like hydrogen cyanide and mustard gas. The most toxic chemical weapons, however, are nerve agents, such as sarin and V agents.

Chemical warfare is not new. In ancient times, battles were waged by poisoning water supplies and adding chemicals to fire to cause more complete destruction.

Modern chemical weapons were introduced to the world in World War I, killing an estimated 100,000 people and causing between 400,000 and 800,000 casualties. While a variety of chemical weapons were tested by both sides during World War I, mustard gas was used most extensively.

Biological weapons contain disease-causing organisms designed to produce sickness and death in opposition forces. Unfortunately, biological weapons have the capacity to severely damage both the human and the natural environment by upsetting the balance of nature. Like chemical warfare, biological warfare has a long history. Ancient stories tell of sending plague-infected bodies into an enemy camp. Today's technology makes it possible to breed germs specifically for use in warfare; unfortunately, the end result is not always known.

It is arguable whether or not biological weapons have ever been used in warfare, but there were numerous allegations during World War I. As early as 1915 reports circulated that German agents injected anthrax bacteria into horses and cattle being shipped out of the United States to Allied countries in Europe. Similar claims were raised throughout the war, although no proof was ever found to substantiate any of the claims.

The decade after the war brought negotiations to stop future uses of chemical and biological weapons. In 1925, the Geneva Protocol outlawed the use of chemical and biological agents in war. Despite this, the major powers continued to develop the weapons, and there were fears they would be utilized during World War II. In fact, nerve gases were developed shortly before and at the beginning of World War II by the Germans.

Nerve agents are feared because of their toxicity. Tiny quantities of these chemicals touching the skin can bring death within a few seconds. The first nerve agents were designated G agents by the U.S. military—G for German, since these particular chemicals were captured in German laboratories at the end of World War II.

Within a few years of the war, the British had developed the V ("venom") agents. The V agents are five times more lethal than the original G agents. The choice of which chemicals to use depends on the desired effect as well as weather conditions at the time of the proposed attack and how long before the area will be occupied. Many chemical weapons disappear quickly and no trace is evident within a few hours after an attack; others remain in the soil for a long time, and it is weeks before the area is habitable.

As in World War I, the use of biological weapons was never confirmed during World War II. There are reports that biological agents were utilized by the Japanese in China during the war. There is also evidence that the Japanese carried out tests on prisoners of war. The United States spent $60 million researching biological weapons during World War II, employing more than 4,000 scientists.

Research during the war focused on anthrax and botulism and was carried out by the Chemical Warfare Service. In 1943, British and American scientists began development of a 500-pound anthrax bomb.

In addition to the anti-personnel bacteria agents being

developed, work was under way by late 1944 on chemical agents designed for use on crops. Documents now reveal that American leaders seriously considered utilizing defoliants on Japan's rice crops in early 1945. Plans were developed to drop ammonium thiocyanate on the major rice crops in Japan. The chemicals were never used—atomic bombs were dropped on Hiroshima and Nagasaki instead.

In the years following World War II, research and development of chemical and biological weapons continued. Chemical weapons have since been used by American military forces, most notably in the form of defoliants during Korea and Vietnam. All of the militaries of the world continue to deny the use of biological weapons in combat, although there have been numerous accusations. Americans were accused of using biological weapons during the Korean War, but none of the accusations have ever been verified. The United States continued to test biological weapons, despite public sentiment against their use. After a slowdown in funding biological weapons programs for many years, the tests were expanded during the Reagan administration, once again reaching $60 million in 1986.

While the available technology and advances in biotechnology make the threat of chemical and biological warfare far greater and more deadly than it has ever been before, the biggest immediate threat comes from their testing, storage, transportation, and disposal. The majority of U.S. stockpiles are twenty years old now. (A few are less than ten years old while others are approaching fifty.) The increasing age alone makes an already dangerous stockpile more volatile and increases the chances that something might go wrong.

Storage of Chemical and Biological Weapons

American stockpiles consist of mustard gas and nerve gases, including the extremely dangerous V agents. It has been estimated that there are 40,000 tons of nerve gases and mustard gas in the United States today. Those stockpiles provide a grave environmental danger. A leak occurred in 1969 in Okinawa, Japan, injuring a large human population. After the incident reached the press and caused a public outcry, some 13,000 tons of the chemical weapons were removed to Johnston Island, the largest island in the Johnston Atoll, about 800 miles from Hawaii in the South Pacific.

Many of the toxic contaminants polluting U.S. military bases today are direct results of the chemical/biological weapons programs. One major example is the Rocky Mountain Arsenal. The longtime manufacturing and storage facility for nerve gas has stored thousands of gallons of the toxins since the 1950s. Waste products from the production facility were routinely dumped on the arsenal grounds. In the mid-1950s, it was discovered that underground water supplies were contaminated and resulted in destruction of crops irrigated with the water as well as the deaths of numerous animals. Officials began to look for alternative ways to dispose of the deadly waste.

In a unique experiment during the 1960s, officials at the arsenal began pumping the waste material into a 2.5-

mile-deep well. One month after the pumping began, Denver was hit with an unusual series of earthquakes. During the five years of the well's operation, over 1,500 earthquakes shook the Denver area. Although controversy continues on whether or not there was really any connection between the pumping and the earthquakes, the well was shut down in 1967. During the five years of pumping, 165 million gallons of waste from the chemical and biological program were pumped deep into the ground.

In addition to domestic animals, an estimated 2,000 ducks and other wildfowl died annually as a result of landing on the reservoirs at the arsenal and drinking the water. The reservoirs have since been closed off so that birds do not land on the water's surface.

Today, there are stockpiles of chemical and biological weapons located across the country. Tooele Army Depot near Salt Lake City, Utah, houses an estimated 10,000 tons of chemical weapons. Another major stockpile is located on Johnston Island. Johnston Island originally contained only the 13,000 tons of chemical munitions received from Okinawa in 1971. Since that time, however, the stockpile has grown as the holdings from Germany were also transferred to that site.

Testing Chemical and Biological Weapons

Another hazard arises as a result of testing the chemical and biological weapons. The most well-known case of this was at Dugway Proving Ground in Utah in 1968. In early 1968, a small amount of VX nerve agent escaped Dugway during testing. As far as forty-five miles away, sheep began to die. As a result of the accidental release, 4,377 sheep died and another 1,877 were disabled. Wild animals that died in the area were never counted, or at least the statistics were never made public.

Anthrax bombs were tested on the British island of Gruinard during World War II. After decades of attempting to decontaminate the island, anthrax spores were still detectable in a 1979 survey. These incidents illustrate one of the problems with chemical weapons. While the levels of toxicity in the air dissipate quickly following contamination, amounts in vegetation remain high for some time. While this is not likely to harm the vegetation, the animals feeding on the plants are in danger of being infected even after the airborne particles are no longer detectable.

Another major problem with testing chemical and biological weapons is the uncertainty of the outcome. French tests in 1952 involved inoculating a few rabbits with myxomatosis—a viral disease known only to rabbits. The disease got out of hand and spread across Europe, ravaging the rabbit population.

Transportation and Disposal of Chemical and Biological Weapons

A major problem facing the military today, and a threat that even the military acknowledges is perhaps the gravest of all, is the transportation and disposal of chemical and biological munitions.

One of the earliest methods of disposing of chemical

weapons was by dumping them at sea. At the end of both world wars, Germany was ordered to dump stockpiles of chemical agents into the Baltic Sea. There was mustard gas at the end of World War I and various other chemical agents, including nerve gas, at the end of World War II. As was discussed earlier, these canisters of chemical agents continue to contaminate waters, plant life, and fish, in addition to killing humans coming into contact with the agents.

The United States buried 1,706 concrete "coffins" at sea during 1967 and 1968. The concrete containers were each filled with thirty rockets containing nerve agents and were dumped in the Atlantic Ocean off the New Jersey coast. Then in 1970, the army disposed of two trainloads of nerve gas–filled rockets by sinking them in an old U.S. Navy Liberty ship, 300 miles off the Florida coast in 16,000 feet of water. Finally, the Marine Protection Research and Sanctuaries Act of 1972 made it illegal to dump chemical and biological agents at sea.

Numerous other disposal techniques have been tried over the years, but efforts became serious following the passage of the DoD Authorization Act of 1986 by Congress. The Act mandated that DoD destroy all biological and chemical stockpiles by the end of September 1994. The act was amended in 1988 to allow the extension of the deadline to 1997.

The Johnston Atoll Chemical Agent Disposal System (JACADS) was completed in 1988—a giant incinerator on the South Pacific Island designed to destroy those stockpiles. Due to the difficulty of transporting the weapons and the fact that stockpiles exist at locations across the

United States, eight additional spots have been designated for incinerators: Tooele Army Depot, Utah; Lexington–Blue Grass Army Depot, Kentucky; Umatilla Army Depot, Oregon; Pine Bluff Arsenal, Arkansas; Anniston Army Depot, Alabama; Aberdeen Proving Ground, Maryland; Pueblo Army Depot, Colorado; and the Newport Army Ammunition Plant, Indiana.

Incineration by JACADS is not itself without dangers. The incineration process generates low levels of dioxin. Mechanical failures and the release of a small amount of chemical agents into the air in 1990 marked the shaky beginnings of JACADS. Despite repeated problems, the incinerator operated until February 1991 to destroy shells containing chemical agents, sent from U.S. stockpiles in Germany. The process is dangerous, long, and expensive. Original estimates of program cost were around $1.5 billion. That figure has risen dramatically. The army estimates $3.4 billion to complete the program, but the General Accounting Office has placed the figure at closer to $5 billion.

Transportation of these chemical and biological weapons poses an unparalleled threat to both human beings and the environment. While some hazardous materials go by ship, the majority cross the United States by truck and railroad. Most of the major interstate highways pass through urban areas, and the majority of rail centers are located close to urban areas. The material frequently travels long distances, since the military weapons centers are dispersed throughout the country. The possibility of an accident exists.

Although there has not been a serious accident involving the transportation of chemical and biological weapons, there have been accidents involving other kinds of military cargo. One example occurred in August 1984 at a main junction of interstate highways in Denver, Colorado. A military truck carrying naval torpedoes overturned. Although there was no detonation, the prospects are terrifying.

Military personnel have a multitude of undocumented stories involving traffic mishaps on military bases. In several stories, military trucks loaded with both conventional and nuclear weapons overturned on base roads or were involved in traffic accidents. The argument that a serious accident has never happened seems to be a weak excuse, since one accident would be too many. The loss to the environment would be tragic; the loss to human life would be inexcusable.

One of the major problems that still exists with the transportation of military cargo, in particular chemical/ biological and nuclear weapons, is that the shipments remained shrouded in secrecy. Various states and the cities and towns through which the materials pass usually have no prior knowledge of the shipments. An exception was made, hopefully reflecting a new attitude on the part of the military, when the chemical weapons stockpiled in Germany were moved to Johnston Atoll in the South Pacific for incineration. Although specific dates and times were not released, for obvious security reasons, the public was informed of the decision.

Experts agree that the most dangerous part of the disposal process was the transfer of the munitions from Europe to the South Pacific. The shells were transported twenty-eight miles by truck convoy to a railroad. The shells then went by rail to an American-controlled ammunition-handling dock on the Weser River. At the dock, the containers of shells were loaded on U.S. Navy ships for a six-week trip to the South Pacific. Eventually, the JACADS facility in the Johnston Atoll received the 100,000 artillery shells in 1990.

Despite military disclosure, there was a loud public outcry by citizens throughout the world. Official protests were lodged by governments in Europe and the South Pacific. The opposition to the plan shows that the public is not comfortable with these shipments and the possible dangers are a terrifying prospect.

In a conversation in early 1992, Colonel Ken Cornelius from the Office of the Deputy Assistant Secretary of Defense (Environment) confirmed the problems confronting the military concerning chemical weapons transportation and disposal. Colonel Cornelius called the transportation and disposal of the chemicals "a real fishbowl operation. Nobody's moving anything or doing anything unless everybody knows about it, because of all the public concerns. And rightfully so, I mean, it's appropriate. That stuff's dangerous. There are no *if*s, *and*s, or *but*s about it."

While conventional weapons and the chemical and biological weapons of today hold terrifying prospects for humanity, nuclear weapons provide the ultimate apocalyptic scenario for humankind. While entire books could be, and indeed have been, written about the threat of nuclear war, the production, storage, shipping, and testing of nuclear weapons are not always considered. The next section focuses on those aspects of America's nuclear weapons program, not to minimize the massive and terrifying consequences of nuclear war but to study the deadly consequences of even preparing for such a war.

NUCLEAR WEAPONS PROGRAM

Production

The U.S. nuclear arsenal came into existence following World War II, and throughout the Cold War, the U.S. nuclear stockpile grew rapidly. The production and storage of nuclear weapons, along with disposal of radioactive by-products and transportation of nuclear materials, brought terrifying new questions for which answers were not always available.

The nuclear weapons program of the Department of Energy (DOE), which consists of testing, design, and production of nuclear weapons, comprises 280 facilities located at 20 sites across the United States. Those facilities are home to an abundance of leaks, spills, and the release of hazardous material into the air, land, and water. The DOE estimates it will take $35 to $63 billion to correct existing problems and to raise the existing standards to meet current federal and state regulations. Other estimates put that cleanup figure at closer to $100 billion.

The most contaminated of all facilities is the Hanford Reservation in southeastern Washington. Hanford has been operating as a plutonium production facility since 1943, the dawn of the nuclear age. Most of Hanford's contamination falls into the category of radioactive waste and includes everything from spent fuel to clothing worn by workers.

Radioactive-contaminated water has been dumped at Hanford for nearly fifty years. As a result, underground contamination now extends at least six miles from the facility into the Columbia River. Test results show radioactive contamination as far away as Pasco, some thirty miles downriver from Hanford. An underground aquifer has also been contaminated. The total amount of radioactive waste dumped over the years at Hanford is staggering. As of 1984, over 18 million cubic feet of low-level waste, 3.9 million cubic feet of plutonium-contaminated waste, and 8 million cubic feet of high-level waste are buried at the site.

The biggest environmental risk in the production process is liquid wastes. Even at the beginning of the nuclear weapons program, scientists at the Manhattan Project warned about the dangers of liquid waste. In an effort to provide an interim storage solution at a time of war, scientists developed tanks to hold the liquid until a satisfactory disposal method could be developed. Although stainless steel tanks were suggested, carbon-steel tanks were used due to wartime shortages. To avoid dissolving the carbon steel, water and lye were added to neutralize the acid content in the radioactive waste. Unfortunately, the interim method of storage became the long-term method. It was discovered later that lye causes a chemical reaction that in turn heats up the tank, finally leading to cracking and leaking. Despite these problems, officials at Hanford continue to use carbon-steel tanks for storage.

As an alternative to tanks, low-level radioactive wastes were routinely dumped into the groundwater and soil. In fact, an estimated 200 billion gallons of radioactive wastes were dumped into shallow ponds and basins or buried in pits at Hanford. An additional 15 million gallons of high-level radioactive wastes were pumped into the groundwater at Hanford in the 1940s.

There is also evidence that the wind has picked up and spread radiation beyond the confines of the facility. Levels of radioactive particles have been discovered in tumbleweed, ducks, rabbits, coyotes, frogs, and turtles.

The initial five-year cleanup for Hanford will cost $2.8 billion, but DOE expects the final cleanup to take thirty years and cost $28 to $47 billion.

Hanford is not the only site contaminated with wastes from the nuclear industry. General Accounting Office officials testified before Congress in 1989 that there are 3,000 individual sites of contamination at DOE facilities. Some of the biggest problems include groundwater contamination at the Rocky Flats plant in Colorado, liquid releases at the Pantex Plant in Texas, groundwater contamination at Lawrence Livermore National Laboratory in California, chromium air emissions from the Portsmouth Uranium Enrichment Complex at Piketon, Ohio, and contamination of the floodplain lying beyond the borders of the Y-12 plant in Oak Ridge, Tennessee.

At the Oak Ridge Reservation in Tennessee, radiation has been discovered in Canadian geese, white-tailed deer, mallards, and gadwalls. While officials for the Oak Ridge contractor—Martin Marietta Energy Systems—claim that the levels of radiation in the animals are not serious even if ingested by humans, there is still a great deal of concern about the presence of any radiation in the animals, and some experts continue to argue that serious dangers do exist.

Perhaps the most historic of all the nuclear production facilities, Los Alamos National Laboratory in New Mexico, has been in operation since November 1942. Los Alamos remains the major test and design facility for nuclear warheads in the United States. Landfills on the site contain 6.7 million cubic feet of low-level waste and 500,000 cubic feet of plutonium-contaminated waste. Flash floods in the desert site cause considerable problems, when plutonium washes down the canyons.

Another major source of environmental contamination as well as controversy is the Savannah River plant in South Carolina. The Savannah River plant is one of the oldest nuclear plants in the country. The plant began operation in 1952 and is the country's only source of tritium, a substance used in nuclear warheads.

After decades of operation, the plant was shut down in 1988 because of unsafe conditions. Those years of operation, however, caused an enormous amount of radioactive waste. It is estimated that 4.5 million cubic feet of high-level waste and 18 million cubic feet of low-level waste are buried in underground storage tanks at the plant. During the plant's operation, an estimated 30 million gallons of radioactive fluids were discharged annually into seepage basins. Scientists originally estimated that plutonium from the seepage basins would take 1 million years to reach the water table. Unfortunately, levels of plutonium were discovered in the groundwater in only 20 years.

In addition to the radioactive wastes, nonradioactive water heated to nearly 200 degrees Fahrenheit was dumped outside the plant. This upsets the balance of the river ecology, killing plant and animal life unable to survive at the unnaturally high temperatures. Due to the stress such dumping places on the ecosystem, the Clean Water Act banned the dumping of water that had not been cooled prior to release. The Environmental Protection Agency gave the Department of Energy an exception, allowing DOE facilities to meet the temperature requirements at the boundary of the facility rather than at the point of discharge.

The results of the dumping were visible at Savannah River. Between 1955 and 1985, when the C-reactor was in operation, the banks of the creek into which the hot water was dumped were barren. Wooded wetlands along the creek were destroyed at the rate of approximately five acres per year, and fish populations were nearly destroyed. It is difficult to assess the full extent of the problem, however, since the water temperature was classified for national security reasons until the early 1980s.

The plant creates strain on the natural environment in other ways as well. It was estimated in 1988 that the Savannah River plant used 3 billion gallons of water annually from an underground aquifer. The long-term stress this could place on the ecosystem is difficult to measure, but overuse of the water from the aquifer can cause groundwater levels to drop as the aquifer struggles to replenish. This in turn leads to lower levels of surface water and possible drought conditions.

On June 9, 1992, the K-reactor at the Savannah River plant was restarted. The sole purpose of the K-reactor is to manufacture tritium for U.S. weapons that are being recalled from service and stockpiled. During the four years of shutdown, the DOE spent $2 billion to upgrade the plant. Yet even during the shutdown, there were problems. During Christmas week, 1991, the plant had an accident involving radioactive cooling water. More than 150 gallons of the radioactive water were dumped into the Savannah River. Another small leak occurred only two weeks before the reactor was restarted. On May 25, 1992, three gallons of radioactive water leaked from the reactor during a critical stage of the operation. These do not appear to be isolated incidents. In fact, thirteen leaks were reported in 1991 and several occurred during the first five months of 1992, prior to the restart.

The K-reactor will be operated for several months during 1992 before being shut down once again. During that shutdown, the reactor will be hooked into a cooling tower to cool hot liquid before it is released back into the river. The plant will then be restarted in late 1992 for several months. Following that period, the plant will again be shut down and placed in standby status indefinitely. According to media interviews, Energy Secretary James Watkins has asserted that the plant will produce no tritium during any phase of the 1992 operations. The operations are designed as a show of force, to prove to the world that the United States is still capable of tritium production if necessary.

The list continues on with examples of contamination at nearly every site throughout the country. As much as 16 billion gallons of radioactive waste water from the Idaho National Engineering Laboratory were dumped into the Snake River aquifer between 1952 and 1970. Plutonium has leaked into the water supply in some areas surrounding Rocky Flats plant near Denver. The Rocky Flats plant produced radioactive triggers for nuclear weapons.

The Cincinnati, Ohio, water supply is contaminated with uranium from the Feeds Material Production Center (FMPC) in Fernald, Ohio. The FMPC is a 1,050-acre facility located twenty miles outside of Cincinnati that has been in operation since 1951. FMPC was built to convert uranium ore and other by-products of the nuclear weapons production process into material that can be used as fuel cores.

Radiological Assessments Corporation (RAC) is conducting the Dose Reconstruction Project for the Centers for Disease Control to estimate the radiation dosages received by area residents. The Draft Interim Report released in December 1991 states that "since operations began in 1951, uranium, thorium, radionuclides . . . including radon . . . have been released to the environment as part of routine operations or during unplanned occurrences."

Many of the "leaks" that the DOE claimed were accidental were not seen that way by RAC. Rather, RAC termed those releases "episodic," clearly stating their reasons for the terminology. "When a large release is the result of a conscious operational decision, it should not be defined as unplanned."

The facility knowingly disposed of wastewater into the Great Miami River, which runs into Cincinnati. The main discharge point for the wastewater was Manhole 175, leading directly to the river. During the early 1960s, the water discharged to the Great Miami River was continuously measured. This scientific precision makes the findings, which were not disclosed for many years, even more shocking.

The total flow of wastewater through Manhole 175 during 1961 averaged 1.3 million gallons per day, or approximately 468 million gallons of wastewater throughout 1961. According to the RAC study and the data carefully collected by FMPC, the figures were slightly less for 1960 and 1962, averaging 1 million gallons per day for those two years.

The actual uranium discharges made into the Great Miami River for these three years are astounding. The highest amount released was in 1961, when an estimated 16,060 pounds of uranium were dumped directly into the river. The other two years investigated in the study showed slightly lower amounts, at about 12,360 pounds in 1960 and 13,640 pounds in 1962. There was an additional runoff point at the facility that accounted for an additional 2.5 to 3.5 million gallons of wastewater per month, depositing approximately 3,000 pounds of uranium into the river. The figures at this runoff point were less reliable than those taken at Manhole 175, because records were kept only sporadically.

Even when attempts were made to filter the wastewater, the system was not environmentally sound. Wastewater was dumped into waste disposal pits, where the heavy uranium collected on the bottom at a rate of more than 55,000 pounds per year in 1960 and 1961. The water on top would then be pumped off, even though detectable levels of radioactivity remained in the discarded water. In addition, high-level waste remained at the bottom of the pit, a potential problem as the material leached out into the ground.

There were also releases of uranium dust directly into the air. The 1960 to 1962 study period revealed between 9,680 pounds and 15,180 pounds of uranium dust released annually. Sources estimate a total of at least 520,000 pounds of uranium dust was released by the Fernald plant through 1990. Again, the figures are only rough estimates since records were kept only on occasion. There are also ongoing dangers from the numerous waste pits, silos, drum storage areas, and scrap piles still scattered throughout the facility.

The tragedy at Fernald, as at each of the nuclear production facilities throughout the United States, was the level of secrecy. The U.S. government apparently determined that the need to protect the country from outside threats was more important than protecting the air, land, and water on which Americans depend. In a way these policies resemble the paranoia of defeated militaries who sacrifice their own homelands to keep the enemy from getting the lands.

Residents of the areas surrounding the FMPC in Fernald, Ohio, have been collectively awarded millions of dollars, placed in a trust fund to cover the costs of related medical problems. Yet the money cannot restore human life, animal life, plant life, clean water supplies, or remove all the traces of decades of poisoning.

Numerous solutions have been proposed to solve the disposal dilemma. Radioactive soil is to be removed from contaminated sites and stored in New Mexico at the WIPP facility—Waste Isolation Pilot Project. A National Academy of Sciences panel studying the project for DOE in 1987 warned that the stability of the facility needed further examination.

The project went ahead despite that charge and various lawsuits filed against it and was completed in 1989. The DOE has spent an estimated $1 billion on the WIPP and continues to spend $14 million monthly to keep it ready for the initial five-year study if the courts clear the way. The government plans to send 50,000 fifty-five-gallon drums of contaminated soil to the WIPP each year for twenty to thirty years.

Another plan calls for the high-level sludge to be solidified into glass and buried deep underground at Yucca Mountain, Nevada. This site also has potential problems. The designated burial location is a natural low pressure area, which could lead to water seepage and eventual contamination of the water supply.

A less-known alternative is burial of the nuclear wastes at sea. Until 1986, DOE's Office of Sub-Seabed Disposal Research studied plans to bury canisters of radioactive waste 100 feet deep in the muddy floor of the ocean. In 1986, the government stopped funding for the research. Given the problems of land-based disposal that have been discovered since then, in 1991 the National Academy of

Sciences again called for renewed study of sub-seabed disposal.

Scientists conducting the research at Sandia National Laboratory in New Mexico propose to bury the canisters under the Pacific Ocean floor, 600 miles north of Hawaii. The chosen spot is not subject to volcanic activity or earthquakes. The plan would be to send the missile-shaped canisters from a ship into the ocean at thirty to fifty miles per hour. Researchers do not know the full impacts of such a plan. Questions remain concerning movement of radioactive materials should a leak occur—how fast particles could move through mud and whether or not the small animals living in the upper portion of the mud could transfer radioactive particles into the food chain. Other questions focus on how to monitor the canisters and how to retrieve them should it ever become necessary.

Finding a solution to the problem of where and how to store radioactive wastes will not be easy, and no community is eager to accept high-level nuclear wastes. However, current methods of handling the waste cannot continue without a major accident that threatens the survival of both human lives and the environment.

The Cold War extended beyond U.S. borders as well. The former Soviet Union—the U.S. "enemy" during the five decades of unparalleled military buildup—has an even worse record than the United States. From the beginning of the Soviet nuclear weapons program, radioactive wastes were dumped into the environment. The first casualty of nuclear weapons production was the Techa River. When radioactivity was discovered 100 miles downstream—at the point where the river empties into the Arctic Ocean—officials began to look for alternative disposal methods.

The "solution" was to deposit the radioactive waste into Lake Karachay. This lake has been called the most polluted spot on earth. Scientists estimate that a person standing on the shore would get a lethal dose of radiation in less than one hour. The lake is now sealed off from the public, but a drought in 1967 demonstrated that man can never completely control nature. Drought conditions dried out the lake and hot winds blew radioactive dust for miles, contaminating an estimated 41,000 people. In addition to dangers at the surface, it has been estimated that 93 percent of the radioactivity is now in the soil under the lake bed and 60 percent of that amount is in the groundwater. Radioactivity has been detected in the ground more than two miles from the lake.

Other methods of disposal proved to be equally dangerous to both human and natural environments. In 1991, officials admitted that nuclear waste had been dumped off the coast of Murmansk into the Barents Sea for over thirty years. The spot is only a few hundred miles from the Norwegian coast in an area used for commercial fishing. Norway has demanded that the former Soviet navy clean up the waste materials.

In 1953, the Soviet Union constructed reprocessing plants and began storing highly radioactive wastes in steel tanks. In 1957, the cooling mechanism at the Chelyabinsk site failed. Material inside the tanks gradually heated up over several days and, on September 29, an explosion occurred that emitted huge amounts of radioactive material into the air. Winds spread contamination over an area

19 miles wide and 150 miles long. An estimated 500,000 people were exposed to radiation and surrounding land and water were contaminated. It has now been revealed that over the eighteen months following the explosion, every pine tree in an area of 20 square kilometers died.

The situation has never improved. There are still large stores of unprocessed radioactive waste in holding tanks. An estimated 600 million curies of high-level nuclear wastes are stored in liquid form along with an additional 500,000 tons of solid waste. The lakes used as holding tanks are leaking radioactivity into the groundwater and there is no alternative available in Russia.

The problem does not belong to Russia alone. The Soviet Union no longer exists and, while U.S. officials are eager to take credit for the breakup of Communism there, they are not ready to help clean up the remains of the Cold War. Unfortunately, in an isolated ecosystem defined by specific boundaries—such as the one we live in here on Earth—poisons cannot be isolated. Substances that poison portions of the globe may eventually poison the entire system.

Nuclear Testing

Another severe environmental threat results from the testing of nuclear weapons. Weapons testing in the United States has generally taken place in the West, on various Pacific Islands, and in the deep waters of the Pacific.

Between 1946 and 1958, the U.S. conducted sixty-six tests on Eniwetok Atoll and Bikini Atoll in the Marshall

Islands. Bikini Atoll is made up of thirty-six islets on a mile-long reef. Eniwetok is a circular atoll of some forty islets stretching for fifty miles around a lagoon. Twelve of the islets in the two atolls were either completely destroyed or left permanently uninhabitable as a result of the tests, and the islands are still highly radioactive. Bikini Atoll, once lined with coconut palms and covered with breadfruit and pandanus trees, is now covered with scrub vegetation. The trees left have fruit too radioactive for human consumption. Even the new trees planted by the U.S. government contain a level of radiation too high for human consumption. There is radiation present three to four inches below the surface of the soil.

Explosions in the water surrounding the atoll caused additional damage. Several small islets were completely vaporized. As a result of the radioactive fallout in the waves hitting the beaches and occasionally washing up over the tiny islands, all animal life on Bikini, except one species of rat, died out.

For a brief period in the 1970s, the Bikinians were allowed to return to their homeland. After millions of dollars were spent to resettle the island, and drastic measures such as removing two inches of topsoil, hauling in barrels of clean soil from Nevada, and instituting massive replanting projects, doctors discovered that the food and vegetation grown on the atoll, as well as the fish living in the lagoons and the water supplies on the islets, were still radioactive. The people were again evacuated.

In Roger Rosenblatt's book, *Witness: The World Since Hiroshima,* he interviews Harold M. Agnew. Agnew was a young physicist working in the nuclear weapons program at the time of the bombing of Hiroshima and Nagasaki. Now retired, Agnew worked in the industry his entire life. He tells Rosenblatt of the perfect plan he has devised to make the world's leaders aware of the power of nuclear weapons: the leaders would stand twenty-five miles away from the test site during a detonation and feel the intense heat radiated by the bomb. That experience alone would demonstrate the intense power of nuclear weapons, and Agnew felt sure it would make any leader reconsider the use of such power.

In December 1950, President Truman created the Nevada Test Site in the desert, sixty-five miles northwest of Las Vegas. Contrary to popular belief that the test site is in a barren desert, there are numerous species of wildlife, including foxes, kangaroo rats, mule deer, wild horses, lizards, snakes, and bats, along with a wide variety of plant species. The area remains the winter area for hundreds of birds and a feeding ground for thousands. There are estimates that 190 different species of birds visit the area.

The average nuclear detonation of 20 to 40 kilotons completely destroys all plant and animal life for a half-mile radius. Some tests, however, have been felt sixty-five miles away in Las Vegas, occasionally breaking windows.

In addition, the long-term adverse effects of radiation exposure are severe. Often there is cell mutation and, as in the case of palm trees in the South Pacific, the species may never return naturally.

Domestic animals are also in danger. The most striking example is in the areas surrounding the Nevada Test Site. In 1953, a series of tests were conducted that were later connected to the deaths of over 4,000 sheep. There were signs of burns and lesions on the horses and cattle in the area. In a 1955 trial, Atomic Energy Commission experts argued that the sheep died of malnutrition and poor grazing conditions, all unrelated to the nearby nuclear tests.

Nearly twenty-five years later, the case was reopened when evidence surfaced that the U.S. government had suppressed evidence that fallout had caused the sheep deaths. In the midst of the "red scare" and McCarthyism, the end had once again justified the means. Although the negligence was proven in a lower court, the case against the Atomic Energy Commission was knocked down on an appeal. The findings by the higher court indicated that the U.S. government was not liable, even in the case of obvious negligence.

By the time the 1963 Test Ban Treaty stopped surface testing of nuclear weapons, a total of 183 surface tests had been conducted by the United States. Scientists are still trying to assess the long-term effects of nuclear tests in all of the atmospheric test areas. In addition to the obvious results of testing, there is also serious erosion resulting from the loss of vegetation. During recovery, grasslands often replace areas originally covered with trees. Long-term radiation exposure alters reproduction, growth, overall population age, and life spans of plant and animal populations.

Radiation is absorbed and held for long periods in the soil, water, and vegetation, thereby posing a long-term threat to any living thing dependent on those resources. One transmitter of radiation is cattle. If the levels of radiation are high in the grass, the radiation passes easily to the cattle and then on to humans through milk. The

U.S. government routinely conducts tests on beef and milk in the fallout areas, but the results of those tests are classsified.

With the 1963 ban on atmospheric testing, the phase of underground testing of nuclear weapons began. Those underground tests are still conducted today. Moving tests underground did not remove environmental dangers. In the immediate test spot, there is rock compression and fracturing of the earth. Earthquakes are often caused by the tests. There seems always to be some degree of atmospheric release of radiation as well. Groundwater contamination is also a danger. Craters are an ugly reminder of the tests going on deep inside the earth.

Nuclear tests were carried out in the Soviet Union as well. The main nuclear test site was established in Kazakhstan in Siberia. Until the atmospheric tests were banned in 1963, the Soviet government conducted an estimated two hundred nuclear tests. Since 1963, more than four hundred tests have been conducted underground. Unfortunately, tests in the Soviet Union took place in areas inhabited by hundreds of thousands of people, many within a fifty-mile radius of test sites. Scientists point to the Volga River as an example of the devastation tests have brought to the environment. An estimated 70 percent of fish in the Volga are contaminated to above danger levels. Vast areas of land in the former Soviet Union will remain uninhabitable for many years to come.

Nuclear Fleet

There is another aspect of the nuclear program that needs to be examined at least briefly. As of 1990, the United

States Navy had 138 nuclear-powered ships and submarines at sea; the Soviet Union's navy had 565. At any given time, there may be as many as 14,600 nuclear weapons at sea.

The United States has been involved in numerous nuclear accidents at sea, and the potential for even more serious accidents exists. It is difficult to determine exactly how many naval accidents have involved nuclear weapons or nuclear reactors, but official U.S. Navy statistics compiled by the Navy Weapons Evaluation Facility and released to the American Friends Services Committee under the Freedom of Information Act indicates that there were a total of 383 U.S. Naval Nuclear Weapons Incidents between 1965 and 1977. It can be assessed from the various reports available that approximately forty-eight nuclear warheads and seven nuclear-power reactors remain somewhere on the ocean floors as a result of accidents since World War II.

Nuclear submarines are a source of serious concern for the potential dangers. In the Neptune Paper No. 3, "Naval Accidents 1945–1988," which was released in June 1989 as the result of a joint effort between Greenpeace and the Institute for Policy Studies, submarine accidents are commonplace. The study looked at a sampling from 1983 to 1987 and determined that there were fifty-six collisions, one hundred forty-nine fires in the submarine forces, twelve groundings, eighty-five explosive mishaps, fourteen nonordnance explosions, eighty-two equipment mishaps, fourteen heavy-weather accidents, and forty-eight cases of floodings.

One example of the seriousness of a nuclear submarine

fleet recently became news. In August 1985, an explosion occurred in a reactor on a Soviet submarine at a shipyard thirty miles north of Vladivostok. The full impacts of the explosion are not known, but reports indicate that large amounts of radioactive fuel spilled into the bay. More than 215,000 square yards of a nearby mountain were designated as a burial site for contaminated debris. An estimated twenty-one miles of roads were washed to clean them of radioactive material. Experts believe the immediate area will contain high levels of radiation and will not be safe for nearly sixty years.

It seems likely that the size and sheer numbers of these vessels, from all the world's nations, will continue to lead to a high incidence of accidents and mishaps. As long as nuclear weapons and nuclear reactors are a part of the military arsenal, the risk for a serious accident will remain high. To date, there is no evidence that the forty-eight nuclear warheads and seven reactors at the bottom of various oceans have caused any release of radioactive material; yet the future of that material remains uncertain. The extreme secrecy, and again the idea that the end is justified by any means, keep the public from knowing the actual facts behind the accidents and incidents. The United States government must make the information available so the public can make an informed decision.

Aside from the potential dangers of any accidents at sea, there are issues involving the nuclear-powered fleet that will absolutely have to be faced. In a 1983 report, the navy estimated that 100 of 130 nuclear-powered submarines would have to be taken out of operation by the year

2013. What to do with the nuclear reactors as the ships are scuttled is a problem that must be dealt with.

After several years of study in the early 1980s, the U.S. Navy decided that the best disposal method is to remove the reactors from the submarines. The reactors have been stored in huge pits on the grounds of the Hanford plant in Washington. The reactors were removed from the submarines, sent downriver from Pittsburgh via the Ohio and Mississippi Rivers to the Gulf of Mexico, through the Panama Canal, up the West Coast, and down the Columbia River to the Hanford site. The submarines were then scuttled at sea. Officials estimate that the outer covering of the reactors will remain intact for two hundred years and the radioactive material will remain unexposed for one thousand years.

Perhaps the most important question that arises in relation to the U.S. nuclear fleet is whether or not there is a real need for nuclear-powered ships and submarines. The basic concept of a navy, in time of war, is to have the biggest and best naval force to enable one country to defeat the enemy's navy. By its very nature, it is assumed that ships will be lost in time of war. Since this is a basic assumption of the military, the presence of nuclear-powered ships and submarines seems to be a grotesque game of chance. The United States is not alone in the possession of nuclear-powered ships or the ability to destroy ships. Nuclear fleets of the world are serious targets in time of war. Fleets may also be targets in times of unrest when terrorists might be inclined to turn to such obvious, floating marks. The scenario for disaster is something the public needs to be aware of, and the public should be given the opportunity to determine if the risk is worth any perceived benefits.

PART THREE

THE
FUTURE
OF
WARFARE

While no one can gaze into the future and predict the course of future wars, it is important to look at the possibilities. Environmental information is available with useful guidelines for military planners. Precautions need to be taken during training and combat. Even more important, scenarios for future environmental terrorism need analysis.

The military has numerous programs in place designed specifically to reduce the environmental burden of daily activities. Actual effectiveness of these programs and whether the policies are carried out in a spirit of commitment or one of mere tolerance are yet to be seen. Perhaps the biggest key to success in environmental programs is the one thing that will be most difficult for the military: Walls of secrecy between the military and the general public must be removed; the "us versus them" attitude will have to change.

The military professes to share these concerns. In a speech before the Defense and Environment Initiative Forum in September 1990, Admiral David Jeremiah, vice chairman of the Joint Chiefs of Staff, urged military commanders to consider the environment. "Our mission of preparing for war will still come first, but with it should come the need to aggressively eliminate any permanently destructive effects our actions might have on the environment."

Admiral Jeremiah goes on to admit, however, that wherever there are military maneuvers, which are necessary if the United States is to have a military force, there will be some damage. He argues, as does Colonel Cornelius, that war is "inherently destructive." He believes that strict environmental controls can impede military objectives. "Strict environmental controls over civilian industries need not ordinarily interfere with their ability to perform their trade. This is not always the case for the military. . . . We still must train our forces under realistic conditions for them to have a high degree of combat readiness."

Realistic conditions that mirror combat situations have traditionally meant exercises without environmental safeguards and without concern for the environment. Whether this remains the case in the future, unfortunately, will not be known until after the damage is done.

However, each branch of the service does have a detailed environmental program that is being initiated throughout the various military facilities. Areas of concentration are: education of the troops, reduction of hazardous materials, reduction of solid waste, and better land management policies.

The U.S. Marine Corps has perhaps the most intensive of all programs, outlined in a Marine Corps publication titled *Environmental Campaign Plan.* By 1995, the corps plans to reduce all solid waste by 50 percent. By the year 2000, the corps plans to have reduced chlorofluorocarbons (CFCs) and halon procurement by 100 percent over 1991 levels. There is also a plan to "achieve sustainable reduction in hazardous waste generation which approaches zero discharge" by the year 2000.

The navy's main focus, according to the navy's publication *Environmental Program: Meeting the Challenge,* is on waste reduction. To meet the goal of 50 percent reduction in solid waste by October 1992, the navy has developed numerous new waste management techniques. One of the most interesting projects is the Norfolk Naval Shipyard Refuse-to-Energy Plant in Norfolk, Virginia. The Refuse Derived Fuel Plant, operated by the Southeastern Public Service Authority of Virginia, receives, separates, processes, and shreds recyclables from seven cities in the Norfolk area. Shredded material, consisting of paper, food, wood, and other products, is then turned into a refuse-derived fuel. That refuse-derived fuel is then transformed at the navy's Refuse-to-Energy plant into steam and electricity for the Norfolk naval shipyard.

Concern for solid waste is reflected at nearly all military facilities. Recycling programs are actively carried out at numerous bases and are often joint programs with the local communities.

The Legacy Resource Management Program is a military-wide program designed to identify and manage significant biological, geophysical, cultural, and historical resources on Department of Defense lands and facilities. The program's three facets are stewardship, leadership, and partnership. There are currently projects under way in thirty states as well as Guam and the District of Columbia. To help develop the Legacy program, the Department of Defense has partnered with numerous federal agencies, such as the National Park Service, Smithsonian Institution, U.S. Bureau of Land Management, U.S. Fish and Wildlife Service, and the U.S. Forest Service. Other partners have included various state agencies, local agencies, private organizations, a number of large universities, several museums, Native American groups, and various private groups and individuals.

A total of ninety-eight projects are currently under way. Among them:

- Riparian study at Vandenberg Air Force Base, California. DoD has a contract with The Nature Conservancy to study and prepare an area management plan.
- Study of a nineteenth-century African-American settlement at Yorktown Naval Weapons Station, Virginia.
- Development of a nature trail for the handicapped at Eglin Air Force Base, Florida. The trail will include interpretive signing to help deaf and blind visitors "see" and "hear" nature along the trail.

- Restoration of 2,000 acres of wetlands at Barksdale Air Force Base, Louisiana, in conjunction with the U.S. Fish and Wildlife Service.
- Development of a boardwalk nature trail over a scenic marine marsh at Langley Air Force Base, Virginia.
- A waterfowl and wildlife viewing area, at Clam Lagoon, on Adak Island Naval Air Station, Alaska, in partnership with the U.S. Fish and Wildlife Service and Ducks Unlimited.

All of these environmentally conscious activities on military bases in the United States and at American bases overseas are impressive. The DoD is quick to send out information concerning what Secretary of Defense Dick Cheney, in a 1989 memorandum to the secretaries of the various military departments, termed "environmental success stories." Yet the majority of these remain focused on the nonmission activities of the bases: the exchanges, commissaries, recreation facilities, family housing. The real test of military commitment to environmental policies in the future will be the combat components of the plans.

Fortunately, there is growing discussion of the need to "eliminate or reduce the production of hazardous wastes and other environmentally harmful emissions." One area where this is being examined is in the acquisitions of new weapons sytems and in modifications to existing systems. In the past, the military called for new systems and defense contractors met those specifications utilizing any materials available. Often the long-term consequences of utilizing or producing the systems were detrimental to the environment. An example is the depleted uranium projectiles. Although purchased for use by the military a couple of decades ago, no thought was given to the effects and possible environmental and health dangers of using the projectiles until the 1990s. The study now would not have been necessary if the military had considered the possible outcomes during the acquisition process.

All of that appears to be changing in today's military. DoD has instructed every potential contractor to consider the use and final disposal of hazardous materials during the development and acquisition process. This was the result of a July 1989 directive from the Secretary of Defense that widened the responsibilities the armed services must take toward the environment. According to the July 1989 directive, in the weapons system procurement process, "life-cycle cost estimates must include the cost of acquiring, handling, using and disposing of any hazardous or potentially hazardous materials. When the use of hazardous materials cannot be avoided, action must be taken to identify, track, store, handle, and dispose of the materials and equipment in a safe and non-polluting manner."

The military still has a long way to go, and much of it will need to be psychological change. There needs to be a more standardized method of overseeing environmental controls. According to the DoD report *Environmental Considerations During Weapons Systems Acquisitions*, which was presented to Congress in late 1991, the military acknowledges this need. "DoD still needs to establish the permanent organizational infrastructure to approach environmental issues systematically, eliminate both inter- and intraservices redundancy, and transfer environmental technical achievements to the benefit of all components and other Federal agencies."

The power and secrecy of the military throughout the Cold War years still permeate defense policy. Even in discussions of improving DoD's environmental record, there is a hesitation to admit wrongdoing. In the 1991 report on changes to the acquisition policy, the reluctance is obvious. "Like private industry, DoD has a large industrial base, which utilizes large amounts of industrial chemicals. Although, in the past, wastes from these operations were disposed of by the commonly accepted practices of the time, we have found that such practices may have resulted in significant risk to public health and the environment."

Beyond changing waste management policies and instituting new environmentally conscious guidelines, the military leaders and foreign policy experts must begin to realize the growing importance of environmental concerns. During World War II, the Korean War, and even during the Vietnam conflict, the public world was not generally concerned with the environment. But if the growing realization that the environment must become a priority is paired with the growing ability to make the environment suffer in the form of terrorism, the future of warfare becomes a terrifying prospect. Terrorists have long known that it is only possible to instill fear in people (a necessary component of terrorist tactics) if the people are aware of and care about the situation. The public is made aware of the situation immediately and close up. (Pictures of oil-covered beaches, dying birds, and the sound of oil-thickened water were seen by millions throughout the world during the Persian Gulf War.) The public today cares about the environment and is aware of the connectedness and fragility of the planet. The public knows that the threats are possible, that it is technologically feasible today to manipulate the environment. Seeds of fear have been planted. Military leaders and terrorists alike will not hesitate to nurture those same seeds for their own purposes. After all, the end justifies the means in military planning.

Another scenario for future war is to fight to obtain or retain natural resources. There is much debate about the likelihood of this ever happening. Yet as populations increase and resources become increasingly more scarce, tensions may well rise. The United States has long had contingency plans for fighting the Soviet Union for control of Middle Eastern oil fields. Although the American people will long be speculating over why American troops fought in Kuwait, oil was one suggested reason. Water and food are two resources frequently mentioned as objects of future wars. The irony of the situation is that wars fought to retain precious environmental resources would probably destroy them in the process.

Various groups have developed proposals to enact treaties and institute new international laws governing destruction to the environment during warfare. The environmental commissioner of the European Community discussed plans in 1991 to develop a Green Cross. Green Cross would be the Red Cross of the environment. An international body, the Green Cross would patrol areas during war to ensure that deliberate environmental destruction did not occur. Any deliberate destruction would be regarded as a war crime. The plan would have to be hammered out and approved by the United Nations, then ratified and accepted by each individual member nation. Yet there were numerous treaties already in place during the Persian Gulf War that seemed to have had no impact on Saddam Hussein's actions. Would another treaty be able to make a real difference?

It seems that human beings frequently put themselves in situations with few solutions. The ability to manipulate the natural environment will be a powerful tool in future wars. The United States military must ensure that training in peacetime focuses on environmental concerns along with traditional tactics. There needs to be real environmental education alongside the rules and regulations. In-depth training needs to be provided in addition to the five-minute briefings given prior to a training exercise. In most cases, people understand better why they need to do something when the rationalization is explained to them than when the change is forced on them. Some of these changes are already being made. For them to continue, they need the support of people's knowledge and enthusiasm.

In an essay for the journal *Environmental Ethics*, United States Army Major Merrit P. Drucker states that while military commanders have a moral responsibility for the environment, they are still not trained that way in today's military. Major Drucker argues that military commanders view the environment as a resource to serve some military purpose. He goes on to say that, in actual military operations, there is little consideration given to the severe environmental degradation brought about as a result of military actions.

Drucker believes these attitudes stem from the training. Military leaders and personnel are told to do something but are given no moral reasons for taking care of the environment. Major Drucker's argument is that environmental change in the military hinges on education of the troops. Leaders of today's military need to learn the inherent worth of the environment and need to understand the long-term value the environment holds for ultimate human survival.

Foreign policy will need to be reevaluated in light of new environmental challenges, potential dangers to the environment, and the changing world situation. A new policy of cooperation and internationalism is necessary. The "us versus them" approach no longer works when the enemy is bigger than all of mankind. Only through cooperation, understanding, and negotiation can environmental catastrophe be avoided. The secrecy that marked the Cold War years can no longer be justified on the grounds of national security. The U.S. military talks of sharing new environmental technologies with other federal agencies. That concept needs to be expanded so that sharing can take place between the government, the military, and private citizens.

Throughout the Cold War, the world was warned of the perils of nuclear disaster. With the threat of nuclear war hanging over the heads of the world's citizens, life at times appeared bleak. It seemed that humans were bargaining with death and would surely lose. The average citizen had no control over events. Men in high-powered positions held their fingers over the button, threatening the other to make the wrong move. That kind of environmental terrorism could not be countered. It threatened human existence, and humans had no say in their own fate. However, environmental hazards short of an all-out apocalypse *can* be regulated. The men and women in the military, ordinary citizens like everyone else, can be aware of the consequences of their actions. The trial of the three employees at Aberdeen demonstrated that there is a legal duty if not a moral duty to take some responsibility for the actions of the military system. That should extend to every citizen. There should be a sense of responsibility, a desire to make things happen and to change the course of our own lives.

Even without the immediate threat of nuclear war, humanity may face serious consequences as enemies fight wars in which they manipulate the forces of nature. In the end, no one can win and everyone may lose.

There is hope that Lieutenant Colonel Gary Thomas is indeed correct, and that everyday concern for the environment will carry over into military combat. There is hope that the men and women in the armies, navies, and air forces of the world will realize not only their own mortality but the mortality of the only home humanity will ever have. If one's homeland is worth fighting for, surely it is worth preserving. As is this planet—our battlefield, our home.

Appendix A:

A Selection of Pertinent Laws and Treaties

ATOMIC ENERGY ACT OF 1946

Established to regulate the nuclear industry in the United States, both for military and peaceful purposes. This act stressed the need for the development of peaceful uses of radioactive substances.

CLEAN AIR ACT, 1955

Legislates the establishment of National Ambient Air Quality Standards and other air emission standards.

APPENDIX A

PARTIAL TEST BAN TREATY OF 1963

Signed and ratified by the United States; bans the testing of nuclear weapons in the atmosphere, including outer space and underwater.

SOLID WASTE DISPOSAL ACT OF 1965

Enacted to require a research and development program at the national level to develop new methods of solid waste disposal. Amended in 1984 to regulate disposal of hazardous waste, to regulate burning of hazardous waste, to require groundwater monitoring, and to detail requirements of inspections. (The Amendment also established a National Groundwater Commission.)

NONPROLIFERATION TREATY OF 1968

Signed and ratified by the United States; prohibits any country from helping any other country acquire nuclear weapons or the equipment that might be used in the manufacture of nuclear weapons.

NATIONAL ENVIRONMENTAL POLICY ACT OF 1969

Helped to establish the United States environmental policy. Designed to encourage harmony with the environment, to eliminate environmental damage, and to lead to beneficial environmental uses without degradation and destruction. Led to the establishment, in 1970, of the Environmental Protection Agency and the National Oceanic and Atmospheric Administration.

CLEAN WATER ACT, 1972

Regulates water quality standards and makes it illegal to dump contaminants into the water. (Permits are allowed for limited discharge.)

CONVENTION ON THE PROHIBITION OF THE DEVELOPMENT, PRODUCTION, AND STOCKPILING OF BACTERIOLOGICAL (BIOLOGICAL) AND TOXIN WEAPONS, 1972

Signed and ratified by the United States; ensures that participants will not develop, produce, stockpile, or acquire biological agents or toxins or the weapons used to deliver these agents.

SAFE DRINKING WATER ACT OF 1974

Ensures a safe drinking water supply for the American public. Environmental Protection Agency standards were set to regulate water supplies.

RESOURCE CONSERVATION AND RECOVERY ACT OF 1976

Recognizes the dangers of dumping hazardous and solid wastes in open dumps and landfills. Defines guidelines for the collection, transportation, separation, and recovery of solid and hazardous wastes. Prohibits open dumping of waste materials.

TOXIC SUBSTANCES CONTROL ACT, 1976

Regulates and controls chemical substances. A "National Defense Waiver" included in the act gives the administrator of the Environmental Protection Agency the authority to waive compliance if the president requests a waiver on the basis of national security. (Author's note: In conversations with Colonel Cornelius in the office of the deputy assistant secretary of defense (environment), he indicated that this waiver has never been requested to date.)

CONVENTION ON THE PROHIBITION OF MILITARY OR ANY OTHER HOSTILE USE OF ENVIRONMENTAL MODIFICATION TECHNIQUES, 1977

Signed and ratified by the United States; insures that parties to the Convention will not use environmental modification techniques in war. These techniques include anything that changes the natural environment of Earth through the deliberate manipulation of nature.

COMPREHENSIVE ENVIRONMENTAL RESPONSE, COMPENSATION, AND LIABILITY ACT OF 1980

Also called the Superfund Act; regulates hazardous substances released into the environment and authorizes the cleanup of such substances. Defines liability and cleanup and outlines compensation policies. Enables the government to collect cleanup costs from other involved parties.

NUCLEAR WASTE POLICY ACT OF 1982

Establishes sites and methods for the safe disposal of nuclear waste.

THE FEDERAL NUCLEAR WASTE DISPOSAL LIABILITY ACT OF 1985

Enacted as an update of certain provisions of the 1954 Atomic Energy Act. Defines liability guidelines and compensation amounts and procedures for incidents resulting from the storage, disposal, and/or transportation of nuclear waste.

SUPERFUND AMENDMENTS AND REAUTHORIZATION ACT OF 1986

Defines response and liability guidelines, including penalties, cleanup requirements, regulations, use of government funds, claim procedures, etc. for hazardous waste contamination areas.

NUCLEAR PROTECTION AND SAFETY ACT OF 1987

Oversees and ensures the safety of the Department of Energy nuclear weapons manufacturing sites in the United States. (The Nuclear Safety Board was established by this Act.)

Appendix B:

Important Resources for Further Information

Advisory Council of Hazardous Substances Research and Training
National Institutes of Health
9000 Rockville Pike, Building 1
Bethesda, MD 20892

Asian and Pacific Americans for Nuclear Awareness (APANA)
6181 Sylvan Drive
Santa Susana, CA 93063
A small organization founded to educate the public about the uses of nuclear weapons. Special emphasis on the bombings of Hiroshima and Nagasaki.

Citizens' Clearinghouse for Hazardous Wastes (CCHW)
P.O. Box 926
Arlington, VA 22216

Clean Sites, Inc.
1199 North Fairfax Street
Alexandria, VA 22314
An organization of representatives from environmental organizations and industry. Clean Sites helps negotiate responsibility and cleanup settlements at abandoned waste sites throughout the United States.

Defense Environmental Restoration Program
206 North Washington Street, Suite 100
Alexandria, VA 22304

Department of Defense
Office of the Deputy Assistant Secretary of Defense
  (Environment)
Washington, DC 20301

Department of Energy
Office of the Secretary
Environment, Safety, and Health
1000 Independence Avenue, SW
Washington, DC 20585

Environmental Protection Agency
401 M Street, SW
Washington, DC 20460

REGIONAL OFFICES:
1. John F. Kennedy Federal Building
   Boston, MA 02203
2. 26 Federal Plaza
   New York, NY 10278
3. 841 Chestnut Street
   Philadelphia, PA 19107
4. 345 Courtland Street, NE
   Atlanta, GA 30365

5. 230 South Dearborn Street
   Chicago, IL 60604
6. 1201 Elm Street
   Dallas, TX 75270
7. 726 Minnesota Street
   Kansas City, KS 66101
8. 999 Eighteenth Street
   Denver, CO 80202
9. 215 Fremont Street
   San Francisco, CA 94105
10. 1200 Sixth Avenue
    Seattle, WA 98101

Hazardous Material Advisory Council
1012 14th Street, NW, Suite 907
Washington, DC 20005
A council of shippers and carriers of hazardous materials, container manufacturers, and waste shipper and carrier associations.

Low-Level Radioactive Waste Commissions
  Central Interstate Low-Level Radioactive Waste Commission
  Office of Air Quality and Nuclear Energy
  Department of Environmental Quality
  P.O. Box 14690
  Baton Rouge, LA 70898

  Midwest Interstate Low-Level Radioactive Waste Commission
  350 North Robert Street, Room 558
  St. Paul, MN 55101

  Northeast Interstate Low-Level Radioactive Waste Commission
  55 Princeton-Hightstown Road
  Princeton Junction, NJ 08550

  Northwest Low-Level Radioactive Waste Committee
  Low-Level Radioactive Waste Program
  Office of Nuclear Waste

Washington Department of Ecology
Mail Stop PV-11
Olympia, WA 98504

Rocky Mountain Low-Level Radioactive Waste Board
1600 Stout Street, Suite 100
Denver, CO 80202

Southeast Interstate Low-Level Radioactive Waste Management
Commission
3901 Barrett Drive, Suite 100-B
Raleigh, NC 27609

National Oceanic and Atmospheric Administration (NOAA)
Fourteenth Street and Constitution Avenue, NW
Washington, DC 20230

Natural Resource Recovery Association (NRRA)
1620 I Street, NW
Washington, DC 20006
*Affiliated with the United States Conference of Mayors, the NRRA
encourages the development of resource recovery facilities and helps
establish recycling programs and waste-to-energy systems.*

Nuclear Regulatory Commission (NRC)
1717 H Street, NW
Washington, DC 20555
*Oversees the Office of Nuclear Reactor Regulation, Office of Nuclear
Material Safety and Safeguards, and Office of Nuclear Regulatory
Research. Also responsible for licensing and operation of nuclear facilities
in the United States.*

Nuclear Weapons Council
Office of the Secretary
Department of Defense

The Pentagon, Room 3E-1074
Washington, DC 20301-3050
An advisory committee that oversees existing and proposed nuclear weapons safety and security.

Office of Hazardous Materials Transportation
400 Seventh Street, SW
Washington, DC 20590

Scientific Advisory Group of Effects (SAGE)
Defense Nuclear Agency
Washington, DC 20305
Oversees nuclear weapons tests and development; reports to the director of the Defense Nuclear Agency.

Wastes in Marine Environment Advisory Panel
Oceans and Environment Program
Science, Information, and Natural Resources Division
Office of Technology Assessment
U.S. Congress
Washington, DC 20510

GLOSSARY

acetone A highly flammable liquid used as a solvent. It is also used to clean electronic components.

Agent Orange An herbicide used during the Vietnam War to kill plant life and remove leaves from trees (defoliate). Agent Orange is a chemical mixture of 2,4-D and 2,4,5-T. The name comes from the orange stripe painted on the 55-gallon drums that stored the substance. There were other herbicides used in Vietnam, including Agent White and Agent Blue.

agouti A burrowing rodent found in tropical areas of the Americas.

ammonium nitrate A colorless salt used in explosives and as solid rocket propellant.

amtrac   A small watertight vehicle introduced during World War II to transfer troops from ship to shore. (Can also be spelled *amtrack*.)

aquifer   An underground formation of rock through which groundwater flows. The aquifer usually is large enough to store quantities of water for future use above ground.

arsenic   A highly poisonous element used in insecticides and weed killers. Arsenic is a substance that is frequently found contaminating DoD facilities.

banteng   A wild ox native to Southeast Asia that resembles a domestic cow.

benzene   A flammable liquid derived from petroleum and used to make numerous chemical products, including detergents, insecticides, and fuel. Benzene is toxic, and prolonged exposure has been linked to nausea, fatigue, anemia, and leukopenia (an unusually low number of white blood cells).

biological weapons   Biological weapons contain disease-producing microorganisms that are used against enemy forces, civilians, livestock, and crops.

butane   A gaseous material derived from petroleum that is used as a fuel, aerosol propellant, and refrigerant.

chaff   Hairlike fibers coated in aluminum, released from aircraft to deflect radar.

chemical weapons   Chemical weapons contain fast-acting poisons designed to destroy enemy forces. There are a variety of chemical weapons, including irritants, choking agents, blood agents, blistering agents, and nerve agents.

chlorine   A greenish-yellow, highly toxic gas. Chlorine was used as a chemical weapon agent during World War I and was subsequently banned by the Geneva Convention. In even small amounts, chlorine attacks the nose, throat, and lungs. With high exposure levels, death can occur from suffocation.

chlorofluorocarbons Methane and ethane derivatives known as CFCs. CFCs have been used since the 1930s as refrigerants and as propellants in aerosols. Because of the risks to the ozone layer, use of CFCs in aerosol products was banned in 1978. (See **methane** and **ethane**.)

chloroform A liquid used in resins, propellants, refrigeration, and as an anesthetic.

cormorant An aquatic bird with webbed feet and a pouch.

cyanide An acid that is extremely lethal to animals. The acid reacts against the respiratory system, causing death. Cyanide is commonly used as an insecticide.

cyclonite Also known as RDX (an acronym for Research and Development Explosive), cyclonite has the highest detonation pressure of any compound used as a military explosive today. RDX was widely used in Vietnam where there were numerous reports of the adverse effects on soldiers of prolonged exposure to the chemical. Symptoms of exposure include seizures, vomiting, amnesia, and possible coma. Cyclonite, or RDX, is the major contaminant at many ammunition plants in the United States.

Defense Environmental Restoration Program (DERP) The DERP was established in 1984 to oversee the evaluation of bases and the cleanup of any identified contamination at DoD installations.

defoliate To strip trees and plants of leaves, usually by means of a chemical spray. Used heavily during Vietnam. The most common defoliant was Agent Orange. (See **Agent Orange**.)

demilitarized zone (DMZ) A zone established, usually by political agreement or treaty, to remain free of military forces, installations, and weapons. The DMZ is most often used when referring to the military-free buffer zone established at the end of the Korean War between North Korea and South Korea.

dichloroethylene Also known as DCE, this compound is used as a solvent. Exposure to DCE can cause nerve damage, as well as damage to the lungs, liver, kidneys, and circulatory system.

dioxin Dioxins are highly toxic contaminants found in many chemical products. Dioxins are found in the herbicides 2,4,5-T and 2,4-D—both chemicals used to make Agent Orange, which was the major defoliant used in Vietnam. Dioxins have been linked to chloracne (a severe form of acne), nerve damage, arthritis, irritability, sleep disorders, and liver damage. (See **Agent Orange.**)

direct destruction Intentional damage to the environment to achieve specific military objectives, such as burning fields to starve out an enemy, defoliating jungles to destroy hiding places, blowing up oil wells to deny oil resources to the enemy and impede advancing armies, or attempting to modify the weather to bring about specific battlefield conditions.

DoD Department of Defense. This department oversees the U.S. military.

DOE Department of Energy. This department is responsible for the U.S. nuclear weapons program, including research and development, nuclear production, and the management of nuclear wastes.

douc langur A rare monkey native to Southeast Asia. Little is known of the douc langur, because it has not been successfully kept in captivity—four months is the longest this monkey has survived in a zoo. The douc langur was evidently further endangered during the Vietnam War.

dugong A plant-eating marine animal that lives along tropical coasts.

embattlement Also called a battlement, an embattlement was originally the top of a defensive wall behind which troops could hide. The embattlement had holes or low places through which guns, arrows, or cannon could be shot. Later, it became the earthen walls built along a defensive line and used for the same purpose by ground troops.

ethane   An odorless gas used as a fuel and in refrigeration.

fluorine   A pale yellow gas that can be toxic if high concentrations reach the water supply. Fluorine compounds were used extensively during World War II in the uranium enrichment process and in the production of high-octane aviation fuel. Fluorine is still used today in rocket propellant systems.

fragmentation bomb   An antipersonnel bomb that scatters shrapnel over a large area when it explodes.

G agents   The G agents were the first nerve agents, developed by the Germans during World War II. (See **nerve agents**.)

gaur   A large mammal that resembles a cow, native to southeastern Asia.

gibbon   A small monkey native to tropical areas of Asia.

groundwater   Water that is below the earth's surface. A large portion of the American population depends on groundwater for drinking water.

halon   A liquid halogenated hydrocarbon used to extinguish fires. The most popular is Halon 1301, which is used in situations where other extinguishing substances would harm equipment, such as valuable papers and electrical or computer systems.

hydroxide   A compound used in the production of chemicals and petroleum products.

incidental destruction   Damage caused by deliberate acts that have some other tactical purpose, such as digging trenches or blowing up chemical stockpiles.

indirect destruction Environmental damage resulting as an unplanned and unexpected side effect of warfare. An example is when birds become extinct as a result of destruction of habitat, or a tree is killed as flying shrapnel severs its trunk.

Installation Restoration Program One of the two major elements of the Defense Environmental Restoration Program (see page 151). The Installation Restoration Program (IRP) is the component of DERP that oversees the identification and cleanup of contamination at DoD facilities. (See **Other Hazardous Waste Operations.**)

JACADS Johnston Atoll Chemical Agent Disposal System, the name given to the giant incinerator built in the South Pacific on Johnston Atoll to destroy the stockpile of chemical weapons held by the U.S. military.

kouprey A wild ox found in Southeast Asia.

LST A military acronym for Landing Ship, Tank. A heavy landing craft used to transfer troops and supplies from ship to shore.

mangrove trees Evergreen trees that grow along tropical and semitropical coastlines and are periodically covered with saltwater. Mangrove trees are characterized by large, aboveground roots that support the trees in the soft ground they favor. The roots create thickets along riverbanks and other wet environments and play a major role in preventing erosion. In Vietnam, the mangrove trees were frequently hiding places for snipers along the rivers and therefore became prime targets of the U.S. military's bombing and herbicide missions.

margay A spotted wildcat that is found in Central America and northern and central parts of South America.

megapode A bird native to Australia and many of the South Pacific islands.

methyl chloride An explosive gas used for a variety of purposes, often as a refrigerant.

methyl ethyl ketone   Also called butanone, this flammable substance is used in cleaning fluids, paint removers, and lacquers.

MRE   Meals Ready to Eat. The standard meals issued to military personnel in the field. MREs come in plastic pouches and the food is ready to eat with only minimal preparations.

munitions   Weapons and ammunition used by a military force.

muntjac   A small deer native to southeastern Asia and the East Indies.

mustard gas   A chemical used in warfare. Classified as a blistering agent, mustard gas is stored in a liquid state and becomes a gas when it comes in contact with the air. Its name is derived from its mustardlike odor.

myxomatosis   A fatal and highly contagious disease of rabbits. Myxomatosis causes the growth of numerous skin tumors and finally death in rabbits inflicted with the disease. Myxomatosis was unleashed on rabbit populations in France during biological warfare experiments.

napalm   A jellylike mixture of various acids and gasoline used in incendiary bombs. This was a popular weapon during the Vietnam War.

nerve agents   A type of chemical weapon, considered lethal with exposure to only minute amounts of the substance. Nerve agents are designed to attack the nervous system, bringing about quick death. (See **G agents** and **V agents**.)

Operation Ranch Hand   The U.S. military's massive defoliation mission flown during the Vietnam War. Operation Ranch Hand, which began on January 13, 1962, and ended on January 7, 1971, sprayed defoliants over an estimated 6 million acres of Vietnam. Operation Ranch Hand was approved by President Kennedy as a method of destroying crops and denying food to the Viet Cong, as well as stripping the forests that provided thick cover to the enemy.

ordnance Cannon and other artillery, along with the appropriate ammunition.

oryx A species of antelope with long, straight horns. The oryx is found in parts of Africa, the Middle East, and southwestern Asia.

Other Hazardous Waste Operations Other Hazardous Waste (OHW) Operations is one of two major elements of the Defense Environmental Restoration Program. The OHW component of DERP targets hazardous waste generation by the DoD. Through research, development, and demonstration programs, DoD makes efforts to reduce and, where possible, eliminate hazardous wastes as a by-product of military operations.

pacas A nocturnal rodent that lives in tropical areas of South and Central America.

PCBs Polychlorinated biphenyls. PCBs were used in electrical insulation until they were banned in 1979 when they were linked to the development of cancer cells in humans.

peccary Piglike, hoofed animal that roams wild in Central and South America.

phenol A poisonous organic compound used in the production of a variety of products, including epoxy resins, detergents, lube oil additives, dyes, preservatives, herbicides, explosives, pesticides, and fungicides. High concentrations of phenol cause skin burns, and it is a violent poison.

plutonium A highly radioactive material used as the fission material in nuclear weapons and as a nuclear fuel.

polychaete Marine worms.

reconnaissance by fire A military tactic popularized by the U.S. Marine Corps in Nicaragua in the early 1980s, while fighting guerrilla forces. The troops approach possible ambush spots shooting, killing any insurgents waiting to attack. In the process, the surrounding vegetation is destroyed by the force of the firepower.

Reforger   Annual U.S. military exercises conducted in Europe, primarily by the army and involving soldiers stationed in both the United States and Europe.

Rockeye bomblets   A 500-pound aerial bomb, containing within it 247 antitank bombs. The American-manufactured Rockeye bombs were dropped by Coalition Forces on the deserts of Kuwait and Iraq in an attempt to defeat Iraqi tank forces.

scorched-earth   The policy of burning off all vegetation in an area to deprive the enemy of needed food supplies. Often, scorched-earth policies are self-inflicted to deny anything of value to an advancing opponent.

shrapnel   Shell fragments from an exploding bomb. Shrapnel can also be small bits of metal placed inside a bomb; upon detonation, the bits of shrapnel are fired over a large area. (See **fragmentation bomb.**)

slurry   A thin mixture of a liquid and other substances that takes on the consistency of cement or a soft mud.

solvents   Strong cleansers used for such purposes as degreasers and paint strippers. These toxic substances were frequently dumped directly onto the ground or into local landfills by the military.

spent fuel   Uranium that has already been through the nuclear reaction and can no longer play a part in the chain reaction. The fuel remains highly radioactive and must be disposed of.

tapir   A mammal found in tropical Central and South America and southern Asia.

thorium   A radioactive element used in nuclear fuels.

toluene   A flammable liquid used in aviation fuels, explosives, and some solvents.

toxic   Poisonous and harmful to plant, animal, and human life.

trichloroethylene   A toxic liquid used to degrease metals and as a solvent for oils.

tritium   A rare radioactive form of hydrogen that can be used in hydrogen bombs.

unexploded ordnance   Munitions (ammunition and other explosives) that did not fire, either during testing or actual combat. The munitions still have the potential to explode.

uranium   A radioactive element that is extracted and processed for use in nuclear fuels and nuclear weapons.

V agents   V agents are types of chemical weapons developed originally by the British. The *V* stands for "venom."

wetlands   A marsh or swamp that remains moist and provides habitat for wildlife.

white phosphorus   This chemical is used in incendiary devices, especially those used for night maneuvers, because burning white phosphorus is visible at night. White phosphorus is one of the chemicals most difficult to clean up at military installations, because it is highly toxic and ignites when it comes in contact with moist air.

WIPP   Waste Isolation Pilot Project of the Department of Energy in New Mexico. The WIPP installation has been developed as a storage site for radioactive-contaminated soil.

SELECTED BIBLIOGRAPHY

INTRODUCTION

Barber, James Alden, Jr. "Ecological Impact of Military Activities." *The Military and American Society: Essays and Readings.* Stephen F. Ambrose and James A. Barber, Jr., eds. New York: Free Press, 1972.

Defense Environmental Restoration Program: Annual Report to Congress for Fiscal Year 1989. Washington, D.C.: Department of Defense, Feb. 1990.

PART I: EARLY HISTORY OF WARFARE

Delbrück, Hans. *History of the Art of War, Volume I: Warfare in Antiquity.* Lincoln, Nebraska: University of Nebraska Press, 1990.

Farb, Peter. *Man's Rise to Civilization as Shown by the Indians of North America from Primeval Times to the Coming of the Industrial State.* New York: E. P. Dutton & Co., 1968.

Jennings, Francis. *The Invasion of America: Indians, Colonialism, and the Cant of Conquest.* Published for the Institute of Early American History and Culture. New York: W. W. Norton & Company, 1975.

Rahman, H. U. *A Chronology of Islamic History, 570–1000* C.E. Boston, Mass.: G. K. Hall & Co., 1989.

Thucydides. *The Peloponnesian War.* New York: The Modern Library, 1951.

PART II: MODERN WARFARE

I. ENVIRONMENTAL DAMAGE DURING WAR

Barnaby, Frank. "The Environmental Impact of the Gulf War." *The Ecologist,* vol. 21, no. 4 (July/August 1991), pp. 166–72.

Beckett, Ian F. W., ed. *The Roots of Counter-Insurgency: Armies and Guerrilla Warfare, 1900–1945.* London, England: Blandford Press, 1988.

Bernstein, Barton J. "The Birth of the U.S. Biological-Warfare Program." *Scientific American,* June 1987, pp. 116–122.

Bierce, Ambrose. *Ambrose Bierce's Civil War.* Washington, D.C.: Regnery Gateway, 1956.

Bowman, Waldo G., Richardson, Harold W., Bowers, Nathan A., Cleary, Edward J., and Carter, Archie N. *Bulldozers Come First: The Story of U.S. War Construction in Foreign Lands.* New York: McGraw-Hill Book Company, 1944.

Chandler, Craig, and Bentley, Jay R. *Forest Fire as a Military Weapon.* Washington, D.C.: U.S. Department of Agriculture, June 1970.

Cornelius, Colonel Ken, and Thomas, Lieutenant Colonel Gary, Office of the Deputy Assistant Secretary of Defense (Environment). Personal interview conducted in Washington, D.C., on Jan. 28, 1992.

Earle, Sylvia A. "Persian Gulf Pollution: Assessing the Damage One Year Later." *National Geographic*. Feb. 1992, pp. 122–34.

Emerson, Steven. "When Earth Takes the Hit." *International Wildlife*. July–Aug. 1991, pp. 38–41.

Environmental Agents Service. *Agent Orange Brief, No. 1: Agent Orange—General Information*. Washington, D.C.: Department of Veterans Affairs, Central Office, July 1991.

Environmental Project on Central America. "Militarization: The Environmental Impact." *EPOCA/Green Paper Number Three*, 1986.

Gallagher, Gary W., ed. *Struggle for the Shenandoah: Essays on the 1864 Valley Campaign*. Kent, Ohio: Kent State University Press, 1991.

Glover, Katherine. *America Begins Again*. New York: Whittlesey House, 1939.

Heneman, Burr. International Council on Bird Preservation. Telephone conversation in April 1992.

Hiatt, Fred. "Governors Wary of Sending Guard Troops to Honduras." *The Washington Post*. April 5, 1986, p. A1.

Johnson, Cecil E. *Eco-Crisis*. New York: John Wiley & Sons, 1970.

Keegan, John. "The Spector of Conventional War." *Harper's*. July 1983, pp. 8–14.

Kemf, Elizabeth. *Month of Pure Light: The Regreening of Vietnam*. London, England: The Women's Press, 1990.

Lewallen, John. *Ecology of Devastation: Indochina*. Baltimore, Md.: Penguin Books, 1971.

MacDonald, Lyn. *Somme*. London, England: Michael Joseph, 1983.

McPherson, James M. *Battle Cry of Freedom: The Civil War Era*. The Oxford History of the United States, vol. 6. New York: Oxford University Press, 1988.

Miller, Francis Trevelyan. *The Complete History of World War II*. Chicago, Ill.: Progress Research Corporation, 1949.

Moore, W. Robert. "Gilbert Islands in the Wake of Battle." *National Geographic*. Feb. 1945, pp. 129–62.

———. "Our New Military Wards, the Marshalls." *National Geographic*. Sept. 1945, pp. 325–52.

————. "South from Saipan." *National Geographic*. April 1945, pp. 441–74.

Morris, Eric. *Corregidor: The End of the Line*. New York: Stein and Day Publishers, 1981.

Nietschmann, Bernard. "Battlefield of Ashes and Mud." *Natural History*. Nov. 1990, pp. 35–37.

————. "Conservation and Conflict in Nicaragua." *Natural History*. Nov. 1990, pp. 42–48.

Pawlick, Tom. "Operation Boogar Man." *National Wildlife*. Aug.–Sept. 1991, p. 29.

Report of Operations of the Cavalry Corps, Army of the Potomac, From April 6 to August 4, 1864. Major General P. H. Sheridan, Commanding. United States Government document, 1864.

Rice, Robert A. "A Casualty of War: the Nicaraguan Environment." *Technology Review*. May–June 1989, pp. 62–72.

Rosenberger, Jack. "War on the Environment: Environmental Consequences of Bio-Chemical Weapons Could Be Catastrophic." *E Magazine*. May/June 1991, pp. 17–20.

Royster, Charles. *The Destructive War: William Tecumseh Sherman, Stonewall Jackson, and the Americans*. New York: Alfred A. Knopf, 1991.

Sheppard, Charles, and Price, Andrew. "Will Marine Life Survive the Gulf War?" *New Scientist*. March 9, 1991, pp. 36–40.

Simon, John Y., ed. *The Papers of Ulysses S. Grant: Volume II: June 1–August 15, 1864*. Carbondale, Illinois: Southern Illinois University Press, n.d.

Steere, Edward. *The Wilderness Campaign*. Harrisburg, Penn.: The Stackpole Company, 1960.

Stokesbury, James L. *A Short History of the American Revolution*. New York: William Morrow and Company, 1991.

Tebbel, John, and Jennison, Keith. *The American Indian Wars*. New York: Bonanza Books, Crown Publishers, 1960.

United States Gulf Task Force. *Environmental Crisis in the Gulf: The U.S. Response*. United States Government study, 1991.

Walters, John Bennett. *Merchant of Terror: General Sherman and Total War*. Indianapolis, Ind.: The Bobbs-Merrill Company, 1973.

The War of the Rebellion: A Compilation of the Official Records of the Union and Confederate Armies. Series I, vol. XL, Part III—Correspondence, etc. Washington, D.C.: Government Printing Office, 1892. (Correspondence between Maj. Gen. Halleck and Lt. Gen. Ulysses S. Grant, July 1864, p. 223.)

The War of the Rebellion: A Compilation of the Office Records of the Union and Confederate Armies. Series I, Vol. XLIII, Part I—Reports, Correspondence, etc. Washington, D.C.: Government Printing Office, 1893. (Correspondence between Maj. Gen. Sheridan and Lt. Gen. Grant, Oct. 1864, pp. 30–31.)

The War of the Rebellion: A Compilation of the Official Records of the Union and Confederate Armies. Series I, Vol. XLIII, Part II—Correspondence, etc. Washington, D.C.: Government Printing Office, 1893. (Correspondence between Brig. Gen. W. Merritt, Commander First Cavalry Division, Lt. Col. and Chief of Staff Jason W. Forsyth, Maj. Gen. Sheridan, and Lt. Gen. U.S. Grant, Aug. and Sept. 1864.)

"War on the Environment and Natural Resources." *Environment.* Vol. 28, no. 1, Jan./Feb. 1986, p. 33.

Weisberg, Barry. *Ecocide in Indochina: The Ecology of War.* San Francisco, Calif.: Canfield Press, 1970.

Westing, Arthur H. *Ecological Consequences of the Second Indochina War.* A Stockholm International Peace Research Institute monograph. Stockholm, Sweden: Almqvist & Wiksell International, 1976.

Westing, Arthur H. "Indochina: Prototype of Ecocide." *Air, Water, Earth, Fire: The Impact of the Military on World Environmental Order.* International Series No. 2. San Francisco, Calif.: Sierra Club Books. May 1974, pp. 15–26.

———. "Leveling the Jungle." *Environment.* Nov. 1971, pp. 7–12.

———. *Weapons of Mass Destruction and the Environment.* A Stockholm International Peace Research Institute monograph. London: Taylor & Francis, 1977.

Westing, Arthur H., ed. *Warfare in a Fragile World: Military Impact on the Human Environment.* A Stockholm International Peace Research Institute monograph. London: Taylor & Francis, 1980.

Wolkomir, Richard and Wolkomir, Joyce. "Caught in the Crossfire." *International Wildlife*. Jan.-Feb. 1992, pp. 6–11.

2. ENVIRONMENTAL IMPACTS
FOLLOWING WARFARE

Aleutian Islands and Lower Alaskan Peninsula Debris Removal and Cleanup. Draft Environmental Impact Statement. Department of the Army, Corps of Engineers, Alaska District, Sept. 1979.

Barnaby, Frank. "The Environmental Impact of the Gulf War." *The Ecologist*. Vol. 21, no. 4, July/Aug. 1991, pp. 166–72.

Bartsch, W. H. "Journey into the Past: Searching for War Remains in the Gilbert and Ellice Islands." *South Pacific Bulletin*. Vol. 25, no. 2, 1975, pp. 8–15.

Benchley, Peter. "Ghosts of War in the South Pacific." *National Geographic*. April 1988, pp. 424–57.

Brady, James Vincent. "Kuwaitis Still Dying from Old Menace: Unexploded Bombs." *Fort Worth Star-Telegram*. Jan. 12, 1992, pp. 1A, 12A.

Cahill, Tim. "Postcard from the Apocalypse." *Outside*. Dec. 1991, pp. 54–60, 108–12.

Canby, Thomas Y. "After the Storm." *National Geographic*. Aug. 1991, pp. 2–32.

Earle, Sylvia A. "Life Springs From Death in Truk Lagoon." *National Geographic*. May 1976, pp. 578–603.

The Effect of Herbicides in South Vietnam: Part A. Summary and Conclusions. The Committee on the Effects of Herbicides in Vietnam, Division of Biological Sciences, Assembly of Life Sciences, National Research Council. Washington, D.C.: National Academy of Sciences, 1974.

Environmental Management Office, Aberdeen Proving Ground, Maryland. Telephone conversations throughout January, February, and March, 1992.

Fritz, Mark. "Germany Digging Up War Junk." *The Denver Post*. Aug. 10, 1991, p. 10A.

Gascoyne, Stephen. "From Toxic Site to Wildlife Refuge." *The Christian Science Monitor*. Sept. 12, 1991, pp. 10–11.

Gist, Ginger L. "The New 'Dead Sea': Persian Gulf Oil Spill Advances Ecological Clock." *Journal of Environmental Health*. Spring 1991, pp. 20–22.

"Gulf War Update: Assessing the Damage." *Science News*. Vol. 140, Nov. 16, 1991, p. 316.

Horgan, John. "Up in Flames: Kuwait's Burning Oil Wells are a Sad Test of Theories." *Scientific American*. May 1991, pp. 17–24.

"How Did Vultures Come to Gettysburg?" *Philadelphia Inquirer*. Feb. 20, 1983.

Jukofsky, Diane, and Wille, Chris, eds. "Conservation in Post-Invasion Panama: Leaders Predict New Era in Parks Protection." *Tropical Conservation Newsbureau*. Aug. 10, 1990.

———. "Nicaragua's Minister of Natural Resources Sees Environmental Opportunities Amid Political Chaos." *Tropical Conservation Newsbureau*. Dec. 10, 1990.

———. "Panama's Former Natural Resource Minister Claims He's a Victim of Political Powerplays." *Tropical Conservation Newsbureau*. June 6, 1991.

———. "World's Most Accessible Tropical Forest Benefits from 1979 Panama Canal Treaty." *Tropical Conservation Newsbureau*. Feb. 4, 1991.

Kemf, Elizabeth. *Month of Pure Light: The Regreening of Vietnam*. London, England: The Women's Press, 1990.

Kolcum, Edward H. "GPS, Other New Technologies Help Clear Ordnance From Kuwaiti Desert." *Aviation Week & Space Technology*, April 27, 1992, pp. 54–55.

Korn, Peter. "The Persisting Poison: Agent Orange in Vietnam." *The Nation*. April 8, 1991, pp. 440–45.

Laurin, Fredrik. "Scandinavia's Underwater Time Bomb." *The Bulletin of Atomic Scientists*. Mar. 1991, pp. 11–15.

Lemonick, Michael D. "Dead Sea in the Making." *Time*. Feb. 11, 1991, pp. 40–41.

McCurry, Steve. "In the Eye of Desert Storm." *National Geographic*. Aug. 1991, pp. 34–35.

Mirkarimi, Ross B. "War Still Pounds Iraqis." *Christian Science Monitor.* June 16, 1992, p. 18.

Munro, George C. "The War and Pacific Birds." *Nature.* Vol. 39, no. 3, March 1946, pp. 125–27, 160.

Nagao, Yuzo. *A Report on Hiroshima.* An unpublished report on a visit to Hiroshima on Aug. 6, 1983, by students and teachers of Yokkaichi South High School, Hinaga, Yokkaichi City, Mie Pref., Japan. Feb. 1984.

Natural Resources of Japan. Report to the Supreme Commander for the Allied Powers, 1946. Report housed at the MacArthur Memorial and Archives, Norfolk, Virginia.

Nietschmann, Bernard. "Conservation and Conflict in Nicaragua." *Natural History.* Nov. 1990, pp. 42–48.

Peck, Louis, "The Spoils of War." *The Amicus Journal.* Spring 1991, pp. 6–9.

Pfeiffer, E. W. "Degreening Vietnam." *Natural History.* Nov. 1990, pp. 37–40.

Quy, Vo. "On the Wings of Peace." *Natural History.* Nov. 1990, pp. 40–41.

Schenck, Lt. Col. Hubert G. "Natural Resources Problems in Japan." *Science.* Oct. 8, 1948, Vol. 108, no. 2806, pp. 367–72.

Schick, Art. "Restoring Damaged Lands." Proceedings of the Department of Defense Natural Resources Leadership Conference, U.S. Air Force Academy, Colorado Springs, Col., Aug. 12–16, 1991, p. 91.

Schmitt, Eric. "Fouled Region is Casualty of War." *The New York Times.* March 3, 1991, p. L19.

Shulman, Seth. *The Threat at Home: Confronting the Toxic Legacy of the U.S. Military.* Boston, Mass.: Beacon Press, 1992.

Slonaker, John J. Historical Reference Branch, U.S. Military History Institute, Carlisle, Pennsylvania. Private conversations during January and February 1992.

Smith, Gar. "Cradle to Grave." *Earth Island Journal.* Winter 1991, pp. 36–40.

"The 'Spoils' of War: Damaged Economies . . . Devastated

Ecologies . . ." *UN Chronicle.* Vol. 28, no. 2, June 1991, pp. 16–18.

Thouless, Chris. "Kampuchean Wildlife—Survival Against the Odds." *Oryx.* Vol. 21, no. 4, Oct. 1987, pp. 223–28.

Westing, Arthur H. *Explosive Remnants of War: Mitigating the Environmental Effects.* A Stockholm International Peace Research and United Nations Environment Programme monograph. London, England: Taylor & Francis, 1985.

Westing, Arthur H., ed. *Warfare in a Fragile World: Military Impact on the Human Environment.* A Stockholm International Peace Research Institute monograph. London: Taylor & Francis, 1980.

3. ENVIRONMENTAL DANGERS OF PREPARING FOR WARFARE

Alvarez, Robert, and Makhijani, Arjun. "Radioactive Waste: Hidden Legacy of the Arms Race." *Technology Review.* Aug.–Sept. 1988, pp. 42–51.

Arkin, William M., and Handler, Joshua. *Neptune Paper No. 3: Naval Accidents 1945–1988.* Washington, D.C.: Greenpeace and the Institute for Policy Studies, June 1989.

Barnaby, Frank. "The Environmental Impact of the Gulf War." *The Ecologist.* Vol. 21, no. 4, July/Aug. 1991, pp. 166–72.

Bernstein, Barton J. "The Birth of the U.S. Biological-Warfare Program." *Scientific American.* June 1987, pp. 116–21.

Bond, David F. "Fernald Contract May Set Pattern for Energy Dept. Cleanup Management." *Aviation Week & Space Technology.* April 6, 1992, pp. 48–49.

Campbell, Christy, and Matthews, Robert. "The Dregs of the Cold War." *World Press Review.* Sept. 1990, pp. 16–17.

Carnes, Sam Abbott, and Watson, Annetta Paul. "Disposing of the U.S. Chemical Weapons Stockpile, an Approaching Reality." *The Journal of the American Medical Association.* Aug. 4, 1989, pp. 653–59.

Charles, Dan. "Counting the Cost of the Cold War Cleanup." *New Scientist.* Oct. 13, 1990, p. 11.

167

Cheney, David W., and Holt, Mark. "Nuclear Weapons Production Complex: Modernization and Cleanup." *CRS Issue Brief #IB89062*. Washington, D.C.: Congressional Research Service, Library of Congress. Oct. 16, 1989.

Christensen, Ned. "Belvoir Grows Around the Environment." *NCO Call*. Sept.–Oct. 1991, pp. 12–15.

Clark, Eugene. "Department of Defense Explosives Safety Board (DDESB) and Its Role in Ordnance Clean-up." Proceedings of the Department of Defense Natural Resources Leadership Conference. U.S. Air Force Academy, Colorado Springs, Col., Aug. 12–16, 1991, pp. 69–71.

Clarke, Robin. *The Silent Weapons*. New York: David McKay Company, 1968.

"Defending the Environment? The Record of the U.S. Military." *The Defense Monitor*. Washington, D.C.: Center for Defense Information. Vol. XVIII, No. 6, 1989.

Defense Environmental Restoration Program: Annual Report to Congress for Fiscal Year 1990. Washington, D.C.: Department of Defense, Feb. 1991.

"Easier Said than Done: Burning Chemical Weapons Is No Simple Process." *Scientific American*. Sept. 1990, pp. 48–50.

Ehrlich, Anne H., and Birks, John W., eds. *Hidden Dangers: Environmental Consequences of Preparing for War*. San Francisco, Calif.: Sierra Club Books, 1990.

Goin, Peter. *Nuclear Landscapes*. Baltimore, Mar.: The Johns Hopkins University Press, 1991.

Grimm, Wolfgang. "Restoring Damaged Military Training Land." Proceedings of the Department of Defense Natural Resources Leadership Conference, U.S. Air Force Academy, Colorado Springs, Col., Aug. 12–16, 1991, p. 92.

Gunby, Phil. "Environment Adds to Challenges Facing Desert Shield Physicians." *Journal of the American Medical Association*. Jan. 23, 1991, pp. 435–37.

Hersh, Seymour M. *Chemical and Biological Warfare: America's Hidden Arsenal*. Garden City, N.Y.: Anchor Books, Doubleday & Company, 1969.

Hilliard, Mark. "The Effects of Tracked Vehicle Training on Wildlife Habitat." Proceedings of the Department of Defense Natural Resources Leadership Conference, U.S. Air Force Academy, Colorado Springs, Col., Aug. 12–16, 1991, p. 59.

Hofheinz, Paul. "The New Soviet Threat: Pollution." *Fortune.* July 27, 1992, pp. 110–14.

Holloway, Marguerite. "Hot Geese." *Scientific American,* Aug. 1990, p. 22.

Kimery, Anthony L. "Base Maneuvers: The Air Force Serves Up Toxic Soup." *The Progressive.* Dec. 1986, pp. 33–35.

Lenssen, Nicholas. *Nuclear Waste: The Problem That Won't Go Away.* Worldwatch Paper 106. Washington, D.C.: Worldwatch Institute, Dec. 1991.

"Military Use of Parks." *National Parks.* March–April 1992, pp. 12–13.

"Nervous About Nerve Gas." *Time.* Aug. 6, 1990, p. 28.

Pope, Charles. "Leak Delays Plans to Restart Reactor." *The* [Columbia, S.C.] *State-Record.* May 27, 1992, p. 1B.

Pope, Charles. "SRS Reactor Restarted: Nuclear Reaction the First Since '88." *The* [Columbia, S.C.] *State-Record.* June 9, 1992, p. 1A.

Radiological Assessments Corporation. *The Fernald Dosimetry Reconstruction Project: Tasks 2 and 3: Radionuclide Source Terms and Uncertainties—1960–1962.* RAC Report Number CDC-2. Draft Interim Report for Comment. Submitted to the Centers for Disease Control. Dec. 1991.

Raloff, J. "Verdict: U.S. Deceived Court in Fallout Case." *Science News.* Vol. 122, p. 100.

Renner, Michael. "Assessing the Military's War on the Environment." *State of the World 1991: A Worldwatch Institute Report on Progress Toward a Sustainable Society.* New York: W. W. Norton & Company, 1991, pp. 132–52.

Rice, Robert A., and Karliner, Joshua N. "Militarization: The Environmental Impact" (EPOCA/Green Paper No. 3). San Francisco, Calif.: Earth Island Institute, n.d.

Rosenberger, Jack. "War on the Environment: Environmental

Consequences of Bio-Chemical Weapons Could Be Catastrophic." *E Magazine*. May/June 1991, pp. 17–20.

Rosenblatt, Roger. *Witness: The World Since Hiroshima*. Boston: Little, Brown and Company, 1985.

Schneider, Keith. "Military Has New Strategic Goal in Cleanup of Vast Toxic Waste." *The New York Times*. Aug. 5, 1991, pp. A1, D3.

Schoenfeld, Gabriel. "Underwatergate." *New Republic*. April 27, 1992, pp. 20–21.

Shulman, Seth. *The Threat at Home: Confronting the Toxic Legacy of the U.S. Military*. Boston, Mass.: Beacon Press, 1992.

———. "Toxic Travels: Inside the Military's Environmental Nightmare." *Nuclear Times*. Autumn 1990, pp. 20–32.

Simon, Cheryl. "Submarine Gravesites." *Science News*. Sept. 10, 1983, pp. 169, 174.

Smith, Gar. "Cradle to Grave." *Earth Island Journal*. Winter 1991, pp. 36–40.

Swanson, Karla. "Tracked Vehicle Training Considerations." Proceedings of the Department of Defense Natural Resources Leadership Conference, U.S. Air Force Academy, Colorado Springs, Col., Aug. 12–16, 1992, p. 58.

Tazik, Dave. "Endangered Species Management at Fort Hood, Texas." Proceedings of the Department of Defense Natural Resources Leadership Conference, U.S. Air Force Academy, Colorado Springs, Col., Aug. 12–16, 1991, pp. 78–79.

Thurow, Thomas. "Tracked Vehicle Environmental Impact—An Overview." Proceedings of the Department of Defense Natural Resources Leadership Conference, U.S. Air Force Academy, Colorado Springs, Col., Aug. 12–16, 1991, p. 58.

Trumbull, Robert. "An Island People Still Exiled by Nuclear Age." *U.S. News & World Report*, Oct. 18, 1982, pp. 48–50.

Turque, Bill, and McCormick, John. "The Military's Toxic Legacy." *Newsweek*. Aug. 6, 1990, pp. 20–23.

Valentine, Paul W. "Aberdeen Officials Given Probation in Hazardous Waste Case." *The Washington Post*. May 12, 1989, p. C5.

Wallich, Paul. "Dark Days." *Scientific American.* Aug. 1990, pp. 16, 20.

Walsh, Barry Walden. "War Games and Multiple Use." *American Forests.* Vol. 96, Nov./Dec. 1990, pp. 21–23, 74–75.

Ward, Henry Baldwin. "Warfare and Natural Resources." *Science.* Vol. 98, no. 2544, Oct. 1, 1943, pp. 289–92.

Westing, Arthur H., ed. *Warfare in a Fragile World: Military Impact on the Human Environment.* A Stockholm International Peace Research Institute monograph. London: Taylor & Francis, 1980.

"What Aberdeen Proved: No Easy Way Out!" *Officers' Call.* Sept.–Oct. 1991, pp. 11–14.

Wilshire, Howard. "Recovery of Arid Lands Used for Armored Maneuvers and Ancillary Developments." Proceedings of the Department of Defense Natural Resources Leadership Conference, U.S. Air Force Academy, Colorado Springs, Col., Aug. 12–16, 1991, p. 61.

Zaslowsky, Dyan, and The Wilderness Society. *These American Lands: Parks, Wilderness, and the Public Lands.* New York: Henry Holt and Company, 1986.

PART III. THE FUTURE OF WARFARE

Barlett, Donald L., and Steele, James B. *Forevermore: Nuclear Waste in America.* New York: W. W. Norton and Company, 1985.

Cheney, Dick. Memorandum for Secretaries of the Military Departments Concerning Environmental Management Policy, Oct. 10, 1989.

Deputy Assistant Secretary of Defense (Environment). *Environmental Considerations During Weapons Systems Acquisition: Report to Congress.* Washington, D.C.: Department of Defense, Sept. 1991.

———. *Legacy Resource Management Program: Report to Congress.* Washington, D.C.: Department of Defense, Sept. 1991.

———. *Managing Postconsumer Waste at DoD Facilities: Report to Congress.* Washington, D.C.: Department of Defense, Feb. 1991.

————. *Waste Recycling Study: Report to Congress.* Washington, D.C.: Department of Defense, Feb. 1991.

Deudney, Daniel. "Environment and Security: Muddled Thinking." *The Bulletin of Atomic Scientists.* April 1991, pp. 22–28.

Drucker, Merrit P. "The Military Commander's Responsibility for the Environment." *Environmental Ethics.* Vol. 11, no. 2, Summer 1989, pp. 135–52.

Gleick, Peter H. "Environment and Security: The Clear Connections." *The Bulletin of Atomic Scientists.* April 1991, pp. 17–21.

Jeremiah, David E. Speech to the Defense and Environment Initiative Forum. Sept. 6, 1990.

Pearce, Fred. "Green Cross to Protect Environment in Wars." *New Scientist.* June 8, 1991, p. 13.

U.S. Arms Control and Disarmament Agency. *Environmental Warfare: Questions and Answers.* Washington, D.C.: Department of State, 1976.

U.S. Department of the Navy. *Environmental Program: Meeting the Challenge.* Washington, D.C.: Department of the Navy, n.d.

U.S. Marine Corps. *Environmental Campaign Plan.* Washington, D.C.: Department of the Navy, n.d.

RECOMMENDED READINGS BY TOPIC

AMERICAN CIVIL WAR

Bierce, Ambrose. *Ambrose Bierce's Civil War.* Washington, D.C.: Regnery Gateway, 1956.

Commager, Henry Steele, ed. *The Blue and the Gray: The Story of the Civil War as Told by Participants.* New York: The Fairfax Press, 1982.

Gallagher, Gary W., ed. *Struggle for the Shenandoah: Essays on the 1865 Valley Campaign.* Kent, Ohio: Kent State University Press, 1991.

McPherson, James M. *Battle Cry of Freedom: The Civil War Era. The Oxford History of the United States,* Vol. 6. New York: Oxford University Press, 1988.

Royster, Charles. *The Destructive War: William Tecumseh Sherman, Stonewall Jackson, and the Americans.* New York: Alfred A. Knopf, 1991.

CHEMICAL/BIOLOGICAL WEAPONS PROGRAM

Clarke, Robin. *The Silent Weapons.* New York: David McKay Company, 1968.

Ehrlich, Anne H., and Birks, John W., eds. *Hidden Dangers: Environmental Consequences of Preparing for War.* San Francisco: Sierra Club Books, 1990.

Shulman, Seth. *The Threat at Home: Confronting the Toxic Legacy of the U.S. Military.* Boston, Mass.: Beacon Press, 1992.

HISTORY OF WARFARE AND THE MILITARY

Ambrose, Stephen F., and Barber, James A., Jr., eds. *The Military and American Society: Essays and Readings.* New York: Free Press, 1972.

Beckett, Ian F. W., ed. *The Roots of Counter-Insurgency: Armies and Guerrilla Warfare, 1900–1945.* London, England: Blandford Press, 1988.

Delbrück, Hans. *History of the Art of War, Volume I: Warfare in Antiquity.* Lincoln, Neb.: University of Nebraska Press, 1975.

———. *History of the Art of War, Volume II: The Barbarian Invasions.* Lincoln, Neb.: University of Nebraska Press, 1980.

———. *History of the Art of War, Volume III: Medieval Warfare.* Lincoln, Neb.: University of Nebraska Press, 1982.

———. *History of the Art of War, Volume IV: The Dawn of Modern Warfare.* Lincoln, Neb.: University of Nebraska Press, 1985.

Dupuy, Trevor N. *The Evolution of Weapons and Warfare.* Indianapolis, Ind.: The Bobbs-Merrill Company, 1980.

173

SELECTED BIBLIOGRAPHY

U.S. NUCLEAR PROGRAM

Bartlett, Donald L., and Steele, James B. *Forevermore: Nuclear Waste in America.* New York: W. W. Norton & Company, 1985.

Bell, Howard. *Justice Downwind: America's Atomic Testing Program in the 1950s.* New York: Oxford University Press, 1986.

Burns, Grant. *The Atomic Papers: A Citizen's Guide to Selected Books and Articles on the Bomb, the Arms Race, Nuclear Power, the Peace Movement and Related Issues.* Metuchen, N.J.: Scarecrow Press, 1984.

Dotto, Lydia. *Planet Earth in Jeopardy: Environmental Consequences of Nuclear War.* New York: John Wiley, 1986.

Fuller, John G. *The Day We Bombed Utah: America's Most Lethal Secret.* New York: New American Library, 1986.

Goin, Peter. *Nuclear Landscapes.* Baltimore, Md.: The Johns Hopkins University Press, 1991.

London, Julius, and White, Gilbert F. *The Environmental Effects of Nuclear War.* AAAS Selected Symposium, 98. Boulder, Col.: Westview Press, 1984.

Mandelbaum, Michael. *The Nuclear Future.* Cornell Studies in Security Affairs. New York: Cornell University Press, 1983.

Miller, Richard L. *Under the Cloud: The Decades of Nuclear Testing.* New York: The Free Press, 1986.

Miller, Willard E., and Miller, Ruby M. *Environmental Hazards: Radioactive Materials and Wastes: A Reference Handbook.* Contemporary World Issues Series. Santa Barbara, Calif.: ABC-CLIO, 1990.

Rosenblatt, Roger. *Witness: The World Since Hiroshima.* Boston: Little, Brown and Company, 1985.

Williams, Robert C., and Cantelon, Philip L., *The American Atom: A Documentary History of Nuclear Policies from the Discovery of Fission to the Present, 1939–1984.* Philadelphia, Penn.: University of Pennsylvania Press, 1984.

VIETNAM

Harnly, Caroline D. *Agent Orange and Vietnam: An Annotated Bibliography.* Metuchen, N.J.: Scarecrow Press, 1988.

Lewallen, John. *Ecology of Devastation: Indochina*. Baltimore, Md.: Penguin Books, 1971.

Westing, Arthur H. *Ecological Consequences of the Second Indochina War*. A Stockholm International Peace Research Institute monograph. Stockholm, Sweden: Almqvist & Wiksell International, 1976.

Wilcox, Fred A. *Waiting for an Army to Die: The Tragedy of Agent Orange*. New York: Vintage Books, 1983.

WARFARE AND THE ENVIRONMENT

Westing, Arthur H. *Warfare in a Fragile World: Military Impact on the Human Environment*. A Stockholm International Peace Research Institute monograph. London, England: Taylor & Francis, 1980.

THE WORLD WARS

Calvocoressi, Peter, and Wint, Guy. *Total War: The Story of World War II*. New York: Pantheon Books, 1972.

Morris, Eric. *Corregidor: The End of the Line*. New York: Stein and Day Publishers, 1981.

Toland, John. *No Man's Land: 1918—The Last Year of the Great War*. Garden City, N.Y.: Doubleday & Company, 1980.

INDEX